EXPLORING THE
TITANIC

First published in the United States of America by Scholastic Inc.,
555 Broadway, New York, N.Y. 10012-3999.

Reprinted 1988, 1989, 1989, 1989, 1990, 1990, 1991, 1992, 1993, 1993, 1993, 1993, 1994, 1994, 1994, 1994, 1996

Library of Congress Cataloging-in-Publication Data

Ballard, Robert D.
  Exploring the Titanic

  Summary: Describes the large luxury liner which sank in 1912
and the discovery and exploration of its underwater wreckage.

  1. Titanic (Steamship)–Juvenile literature.   2. Shipwrecks–
North Atlantic Ocean–Juvenile literature.   3. Underwater
exploration–North Atlantic Ocean–Juvenile literature.
[1. Titanic (Steamship)   2. Shipwrecks.   3. Underwater
exploration]
I. Title.

G530.T6B494   1988   363.1'23'091631   88-6478

ISBN 0-590-41953-6 (Scholastic Hardcover)

ISBN 0-590-41952-8 (Scholastic Paperback)

DESIGN AND ART DIRECTION: Pronk & Associates Inc.

EDITORIAL: Hugh Brewster, Shelley Tanaka, Celia Lottridge

PRODUCTION: Susan Barrable, Pamela Yong

Produced by
Madison Press Books
40 Madison Avenue
Toronto, Ontario
Canada M5R 2S1

Printed in Mexico

EXPLORING THE
TITANIC

by Robert D. Ballard

Edited by Patrick Crean
Illustrations of the Titanic by Ken Marschall

A Scholastic/Madison Press Book

N O ONE EVER DREAMED THAT HER FIRST voyage would also be her last. On the night of April 14, 1912, the passenger liner R.M.S. *Titanic* struck an iceberg in the North Atlantic. Within minutes water began pouring into her lower decks. Less than three hours later her propellers started to rise out of the water. For the more than 1,500 people left on board there was little hope of escape. Soon the biggest ship the world had ever seen would plunge to the bottom of the ocean.

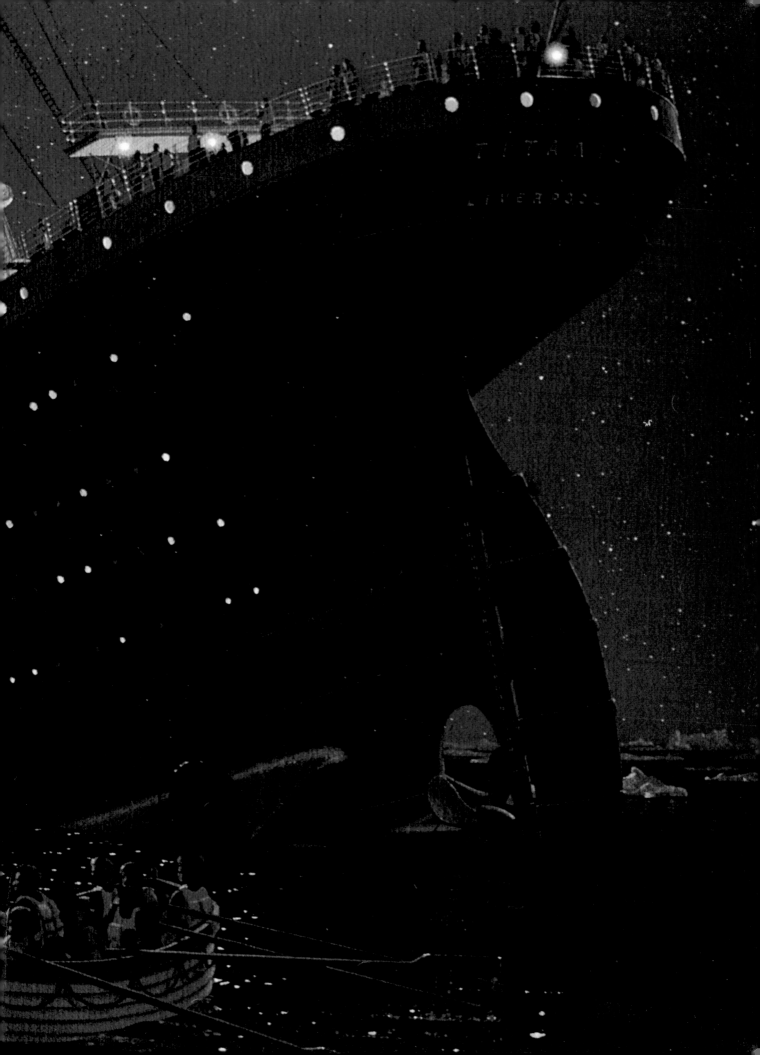

IN JULY OF 1986 ROBERT BALLARD AND TWO members of his team descended two and a half miles to the ocean floor in their tiny submarine. One year earlier they had located the wreck of the *Titanic*. Now they wanted to explore the sunken liner at close range. As they shone their lights on the rusted wreck of the lost ship, the events of that night 74 years earlier seemed to come alive once again.

CHAPTER ONE

The Beginning of a Dream

"I'M SURE EVERY DIVER DREAMS ABOUT THE *TITANIC*," said the speaker at the Sea Rovers meeting. "To dive down to that fabulous ship would be the ultimate thrill in underwater exploration. But she's probably too far down for anybody to ever find her — far less explore her."

It was 1967, and I was a young member of the Boston Sea Rovers, a group of people who loved the sea and the excitement of underwater exploring. Many of the speakers at our meetings were the stars of the underwater world. I had listened to the famous explorer and diver Jacques Cousteau and to Dr. Eugenie Clark, the shark expert, and been completely awed by their experiences. All of the Sea Rovers loved to talk about shipwrecks and the treasures of the deep. Listening to them, I began to dream about diving to the greatest shipwreck of them all: the *Titanic*.

As long as I can remember, I've been fascinated by the sea. As a boy growing up in southern California, I was always collecting shells and driftwood that the ocean washed up on the beaches. I also loved to watch the creatures that lived underwater in tidal pools. As a teenager, instead of becoming a surfer like most of my friends, I took up scuba diving and began to explore the world just beneath the ocean surface. Jules Verne's *20,000 Leagues Under the Sea*, with its adventures of Captain Nemo aboard his legendary submarine, *Nautilus*, was a book I read over and over again.

At university I did post-graduate work in marine geology at the University of Hawaii. To help pay my expenses I worked as a porpoise trainer

Training dolphins at Sea Life Park.

at Sea Life Park. I spent hours teaching dolphins to dive through hoops and perform other tricks.

My schooling came to an abrupt halt when I was called into the U.S. Navy. In 1967 my wife Marjorie and I loaded all our possessions into our tiny car and drove across the United States to Woods Hole, Massachusetts, on Cape Cod. The Navy had assigned me to the Deep Submergence Group at Woods Hole Oceanographic Institution. Woods Hole is one of the world's most important institutes for the study of the oceans.

Although the oceans cover more than two-thirds of our planet, we are now just beginning to understand them. At Woods Hole, scientists study the mysteries of the oceans both above and below the surface — from weather patterns and tides to underwater currents, sea creatures and plants, and the mountain ranges of the deep.

The first time I thought it might be possible to find the *Titanic* was in 1973, when I was a member of the *Alvin* team. *Alvin* is a small three-man

submarine. It is officially named after Al Vine, a veteran oceanographer, but unofficially named for Alvin the chipmunk.

Alvin could only dive to 6,000 feet. Since the average depth of the deep ocean is about 12,000 feet, the Navy decided to give it a new hull of titanium alloy, a very strong metal that could hold up to huge underwater pressures and allow us to dive to 13,000 feet. By chance, this refitting project was called Project Titanus.

Titanium, Titanus, *Titanic*—that started me thinking. The *Titanic* was thought to lie at a depth of just over 12,000 feet. I suddenly realized that I could dive to the *Titanic* in *Alvin*! Now thoughts of the *Titanic* just wouldn't leave me alone. I knew I had to find that ship.

For twelve long years I tried to get people interested in my dream. I made plans and tried without much luck to raise the money I would need to mount the kind of expedition that could find the wreck of the *Titanic*.

During those years I also worked as a scientist exploring other parts of the world's oceans. In 1973 and 1974 I joined expeditions that explored the Mid-Atlantic Ridge, an enormous underwater mountain range running down the middle of the Atlantic Ocean. This ridge is part of an even bigger undersea range that extends 40,000 miles around the world. In 1977, near the Galapagos Islands off the coast of Ecuador, we discovered enormous red worms, some of them more than eight feet long. These giant worms live inside white tubes and cluster around underwater hot springs. In 1979, off Baja California, we made the most spectacular discovery of all—the amazing black smokers. These underwater vents belch out fluids hot enough to melt lead, and shoot them straight up from the ocean floor through chimneys of lava.

Soon I had spent more hours in the deep ocean than any other scientist. But the *Titanic* continued to haunt me. My oceanographic colleagues scoffed at my *Titanic* dreams and told me I should devote myself to "real" scientific projects.

Then I met Bill Tantum. Bill's nickname was "Mr. *Titanic*," because he knew so much about the ship. I would sit and listen for hours as he told me the spellbinding story of what had happened the night she sank. Together we would talk about my dream of finding her. The *Titanic* began to mean more to me than simply a challenging target to find in the deep ocean. This greatest of all sea disasters soon gripped me as a fascinating and moving human drama.

Now the *Titanic* had me completely under her spell.

CHAPTER TWO

The Biggest Ship in the World

THE STORY OF THE *TITANIC* BEGAN BEFORE ANY-one had even thought about building the great ship. In 1898, fourteen years before the *Titanic* sank, an American writer named Morgan Robertson wrote a book called *The Wreck of the Titan*. In his story, the *Titan*, a passenger ship almost identical to the *Titanic*, and labelled "unsinkable," sails from England headed for New York. With many rich and famous passengers on board, the *Titan* hits an iceberg in the North Atlantic and sinks. Because there are not enough lifeboats, many lives are lost.

The story of the *Titan* predicted exactly what would happen to the *Titanic* fourteen years later. It was an eerie prophecy of terrible things to come.

In 1907, nearly ten years after *The Wreck of the Titan* was written, two men began making plans to build a real titanic ship. At a London dinner party, as they relaxed over coffee and cigars, J. Bruce Ismay, president of the White Star Line of passenger ships, and Lord Pirrie, chairman of Harland & Wolff shipbuilders, discussed a plan to build three enormous ocean liners. Their goal was to give the White Star Line a competitive edge in the Atlantic passenger trade with several gigantic ships whose accommodations would be the last word in comfort and elegance.

The two men certainly dreamed on a grand scale. When these floating palaces were finally built, they were so much bigger than other ships that new docks had to be built on each side of the Atlantic to service them. Four years after that London dinner party, the first of these huge liners, the *Olympic*, safely completed her maiden voyage.

If placed upright, the *Titanic* would have been taller than any of the buildings of her day.

On May 31, 1911, the hull of the *Titanic* was launched at the Harland & Wolff shipyards in Belfast, Ireland, before a cheering crowd of 100,000. Bands played and people came from miles around to see this great wonder of the sea. Twenty-two tons of soap, grease, and train-oil were used to slide her into the water. In the words of one eyewitness, she had "a rudder as big as an elm tree...propellers as big as a windmill. Everything was on a nightmare scale."

For the next ten months the *Titanic* was outfitted and carefully prepared down to the last detail. The final size and richness of this new ship was astounding. She was 882 feet long, almost the length of four city blocks. With nine decks, she was as high as an eleven-storey building.

Among her gigantic features, she had four huge funnels, each one big enough to drive two trains through. During construction an astonishing three million rivets had been hammered into her hull. Her three enormous anchors weighed a total of thirty-one tons — the weight of twenty cars.

(Above) One of the giant funnels leaving the shop where it was built.

(Above right) A team of 20 horses pulling a 15 1/2-ton anchor made for the *Titanic*.

(Right) Forging the links of the huge anchor chains.

(Below) At the shipyard in Belfast, the *Titanic* is made ready for launching.

And for her maiden voyage, she carried enough food to feed a small town for several months.

As her name boasted, the *Titanic* was indeed the biggest ship in the world. Nicknamed "the Millionaires' Special," she was also called "the Wonder Ship," "the Unsinkable Ship," and "the Last Word in Luxury" by newspapers around the world.

The command of this great ocean liner was given to the senior captain of the White Star Line, Captain Edward J. Smith. This proud, white-bearded man was a natural leader and was popular with both crew members and passengers. Most important, after thirty-eight years' service with the White Star Line, he had an excellent safety record. At the age of fifty-nine, Captain Smith was going to retire after this last trip, a perfect final tribute to a long and successful career.

On Wednesday, April 10, 1912, the *Titanic*'s passengers began to arrive in Southampton for the trip to New York. Ruth Becker was dazzled as she boarded the ship with her mother, her younger sister, and two-year-old brother, Richard. Ruth's father was a missionary in India. The rest of the family was sailing to New York to find medical help for young Richard, who had developed a serious illness in India. They had booked second-class tickets on the *Titanic*.

The deck of the forecastle area of the ship held the giant anchor chains and large round bollards to which ropes were tied when the ship was in port.

First Class

Second Class

Third Class

Crew Living and Eating Areas

Crew Working Areas

Cargo and Stores

Purser McElroy **(left)** and Captain Smith **(right)** stand outside the officers' quarters.

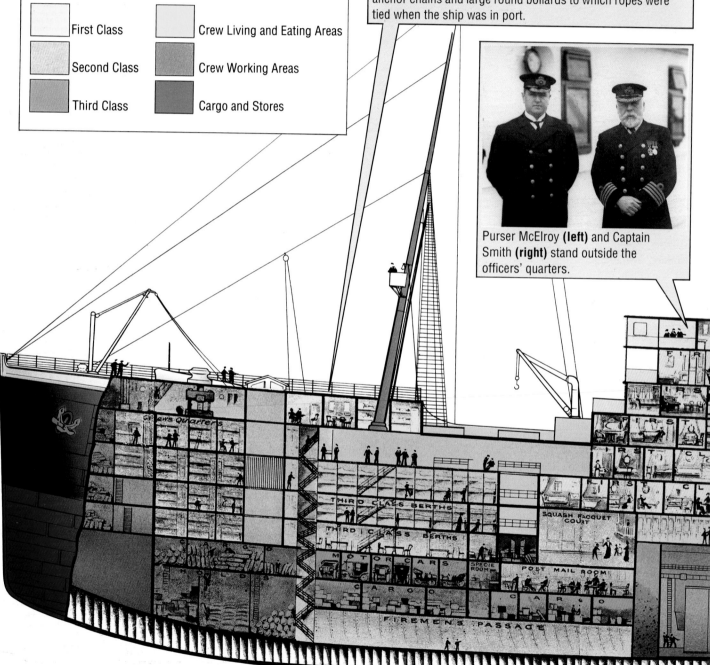

This elegant foyer stood below the wrought-iron and glass dome over the first-class staircase.

Instructor T. W. McCawley demonstrates the rowing machine in the ship's gymnasium.

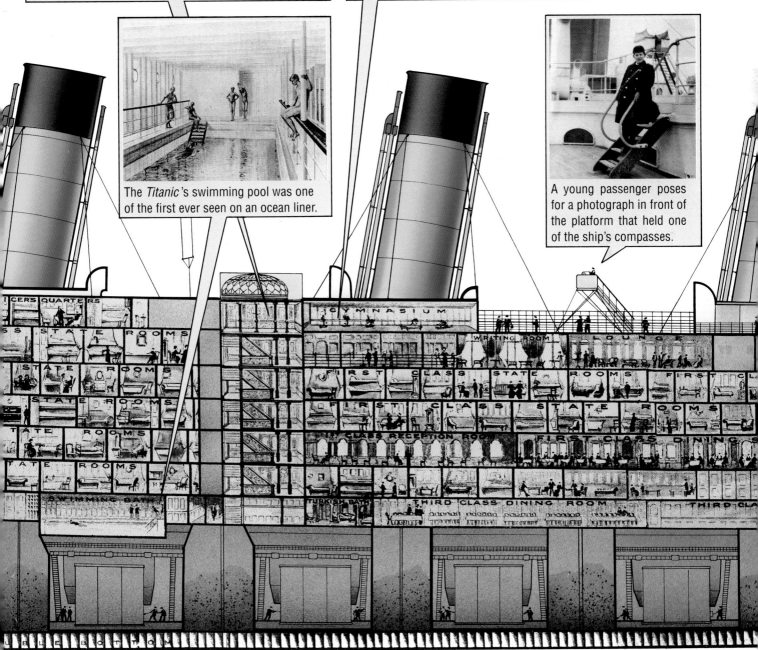

The *Titanic*'s swimming pool was one of the first ever seen on an ocean liner.

A young passenger poses for a photograph in front of the platform that held one of the ship's compasses.

Twelve-year-old Ruth was delighted with the ship. As she pushed her little brother about the decks in a stroller, she was impressed with what she saw. "Everything was new. New!" she recalled. "Our cabin was just like a hotel room, it was so big. The dining room was beautiful—the linens, all the bright, polished silver you can imagine."

Meanwhile, seventeen-year-old Jack Thayer from Philadelphia was trying out the soft mattress on the large bed in his cabin. The first-class rooms

The boilers of the *Titanic* were over 15 feet high.

Stokers worked day and night shoveling coal into boilers that created the steam that drove the giant reciprocating engines.

A mother reads aloud to her daughter in a second-class cabin.

his family had reserved for themselves and their maid had thick carpets, carved wooden panels on the walls, and marble sinks. As his parents were getting settled in their adjoining stateroom, Jack decided to explore this fantastic ship.

On A Deck, he stepped into the Verandah and Palm Court and admired the white wicker furniture and the ivy growing up the trellised walls. On the lower decks, Jack discovered the squash court, the swimming pool, and the Turkish bath decorated like a room in a sultan's palace. In the gymnasium, the instructor was showing passengers the latest in exercise equipment, which included a mechanical camel you could ride on, stationary bicycles, and rowing machines.

Daylight shone through the huge glass dome over the Grand Staircase as Jack went down to join his parents in the first-class reception room.

A six-year-old boy spins his top on the first-class Promenade Deck while his father and two other passengers watch.

The *Titanic* had three propellers. The middle one was 16 feet across and the other two were over 23 feet.

(Inset right) A 1912 photograph of Ruth Becker with her two-year-old brother, Richard. Behind her is a second-class stateroom like the one the Beckers would have had. Against the wall is a washstand with sinks that could be tipped to allow the water to drain out.

(Below) Potted palms and wicker furniture made the first-class reception room a pleasant place to meet friends before dinner.

There, with the ship's band playing in the background, his father pointed out some of the other first-class passengers. "He's supposed to be the world's richest man," said his father of Colonel John Jacob Astor, who was escorting the young Mrs. Astor. He also identified Mr. and Mrs. Straus, founders of Macy's of New York, the world's largest department store. Millionaire Benjamin Guggenheim was aboard, as were Jack's parents' friends from Philadelphia, Mr. and Mrs. George Widener and their son, Harry. Mr. Widener had made a fortune building streetcars. Mr. and Mrs. William Carter were also friends of the Thayers. Stowed in one of the holds below was a new Renault car that they were bringing back from England.

J. Bruce Ismay, president of the White Star Line, moved about the room saying hello to people. He wanted to make sure that his wealthy passengers were comfortable, that they would feel relaxed and safe aboard his floating palace.

Indeed, when Ruth Becker's mother had asked one of the second-class staff about the safety of the ship, she had been told that there was absolutely nothing to worry about. The ship had watertight compartments that would allow her to float indefinitely. There was much talk among the passengers about the *Titanic* being unsinkable.

In 1912, people were divided into social classes according to background, wealth, and education. Because of these class lines, the *Titanic* was rather like a big floating layer cake. The bottom layer consisted of the lowly manual workers sweating away in the heat and grime of the boiler rooms and engine rooms. The next layer was the third-class passengers, people of many nationalities hoping to make a new start in America. After

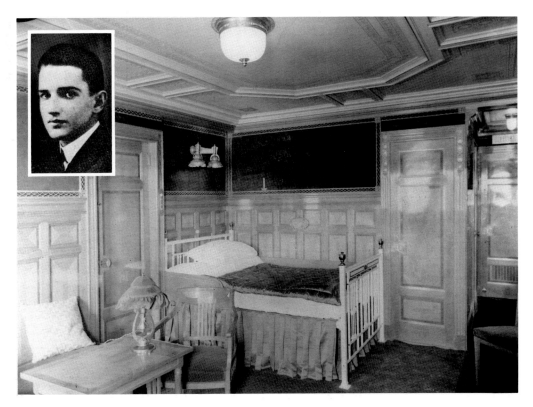

(Inset right) Jack Thayer at age sixteen. The room behind him shows the more elaborate furnishings that the Thayer family would have enjoyed in a first-class stateroom.

(Below) A room where first-class passengers could relax and cool down after a Turkish steam bath.

that came the second class — teachers, merchants, and professionals of moderate means like Ruth's family. Then, finally, there was the icing on the cake in first class: the rich and the aristocratic. The differences between these groups were enormous. While the wealthy brought their maids and valets and mountains of luggage, most members of the crew earned such tiny salaries that it would have taken them years to save the money for a single first-class ticket.

At noon on Wednesday, April 10, the *Titanic* cast off. The whistles on her huge funnels were the biggest ever made. As she began her journey to the sea, they were heard for miles around.

Moving majestically down the River Test, and watched by a crowd that had turned out for the occasion, the *Titanic* slowly passed two ships tied up to a dock. All of a sudden, the mooring ropes holding the passenger liner *New York* snapped with a series of sharp cracks like fireworks going off. The enormous pull created by the *Titanic* moving past her had broken the *New York*'s ropes and was now drawing her stern toward the *Titanic*. Jack Thayer watched in horror as the two ships came closer and closer. "It looked as though there surely would be a collision," he later wrote. "Her stern could not have been more than a yard or two from our side. It almost hit us." At the last moment, some quick action by Captain Smith and a tugboat captain nearby allowed the *Titanic* to slide past with only inches to spare.

It was not a good sign. Did it mean that the *Titanic* might be too big a ship to handle safely? Those who knew about the sea thought that such a close call at the beginning of a maiden voyage was a very bad omen.

CHAPTER THREE

The Fateful Night

JACK PHILLIPS, THE FIRST WIRELESS OPERATOR ON the *Titanic*, quickly jotted down the message coming in over his headphones. "It's another iceberg warning," he said wearily to his young assistant, Harold Bride. "You'd better take it up to the bridge." Both men had been at work for hours in the *Titanic*'s radio room, trying to get caught up in sending out a large number of personal messages. In 1912, passengers on ocean liners thought it was a real novelty to send postcard-style messages to friends at home from the middle of the Atlantic.

Bride picked up the iceberg message and stepped out onto the Boat Deck. It was a sunny but cold Sunday morning, the fourth day of the *Titanic*'s maiden voyage. The ship was steaming at full speed across a calm sea. Harold Bride was quite pleased with himself at having landed a

A wireless operator at work in a radio room similar to the one on board the *Titanic*.

job on such a magnificent new ship. After all, he was only twenty-two years old and had just nine months' experience at operating a "wireless set," as a ship's radio was then called. As he entered the bridge area, he could see one of the crewmen standing behind the ship's wheel steering her course toward New York.

Captain Smith was on duty in the bridge, so Bride handed the message to him. "It's from the *Caronia*, sir. She's reporting icebergs and pack ice ahead." The captain thanked him, read the message, and then posted it on the bulletin board for other officers on watch to read. On his way back to the radio room, Bride thought the captain had seemed quite unconcerned by the message. But then again, he had been told that it was not unusual to have ice floating in the sea lanes during an April crossing. Besides, what danger could a few pieces of ice present to an unsinkable ship?

Elsewhere on board, passengers relaxed on deck chairs, reading or taking naps. Some played cards, some wrote letters, while others chatted with friends. As it was Sunday, church services had been held in the morning, the first-class service led by Captain Smith. Jack Thayer spent most of the day walking about the decks getting some fresh air with his parents.

Two more ice warnings were received from nearby ships around lunch time. In the chaos of the radio room, Harold Bride only had time to take one of them to the bridge. The rest of the day passed quietly. Then, in the late afternoon, the temperature began to drop rapidly. Darkness approached as the bugle call announced dinner.

The *Titanic* as she steams away from Queenstown, Ireland.

Jack Thayer's parents had been invited to a special dinner for Captain Smith, so Jack ate alone in the first-class dining room. After dinner, as he was having a cup of coffee, he was joined by Milton Long, another passenger going home to the States. Long was older than Jack, but in the easy-going atmosphere of shipboard travel, they struck up a conversation and talked together for an hour or so.

At 7:30 p.m., the radio room received three more warnings of ice about fifty miles ahead. One of them was from the steamer *Californian* reporting three large icebergs. Harold Bride took this message up to the bridge and it was again politely received. Captain Smith was attending the dinner party being held for him when the warning was delivered. He never got to see it. Then, around 9:00 p.m., the captain excused himself and went up to the bridge. He and his officers talked about how difficult it was to spot icebergs on a calm, clear, moonless night like this with no wind to kick up white surf around them. Before going to bed, the captain ordered the lookouts to keep a sharp watch for ice.

After trading travel stories with Milton Long, Jack Thayer put on his coat and walked around the deck. "It had become very much colder," he said later. "It was a brilliant, starry night. There was no moon and I have never seen the stars shine brighter...sparkling like diamonds....It was the kind of night that made one feel glad to be alive." At eleven o'clock, he went below to his cabin, put on his pajamas, and got ready for bed.

In the radio room, Harold Bride was exhausted. The two operators were expected to keep the radio working twenty-four hours a day, and Bride lay down to take a much-needed nap. Phillips was so busy with the passenger messages that he actually brushed off the final ice warning of the night. It was from the *Californian*. Trapped in a field of ice, she had stopped for the night about nineteen miles north of the *Titanic*. She was so close that the message literally blasted in Phillips' ears. Annoyed by the loud interruption, he cut off the *Californian*'s radio operator with the words, "Shut up, shut up. I'm busy."

The radio room had received a total of seven ice warning messages in one day. It was quite clear that floating icebergs lay ahead of the *Titanic*.

High up in the crow's nest on the forward mast, Fred Fleet had passed a quiet watch. It was now 11:40 p.m., and he and his fellow lookout were waiting to be relieved so they could head below, perhaps for a hot drink before hopping into their warm bunks. The sea was dead calm. The air was bitterly cold.

(Top) One of the iceberg warning messages that the *Titanic* received and passed on to other ships.

(Above left) First Wireless Operator Jack Phillips and his assistant, Harold Bride **(right)**.

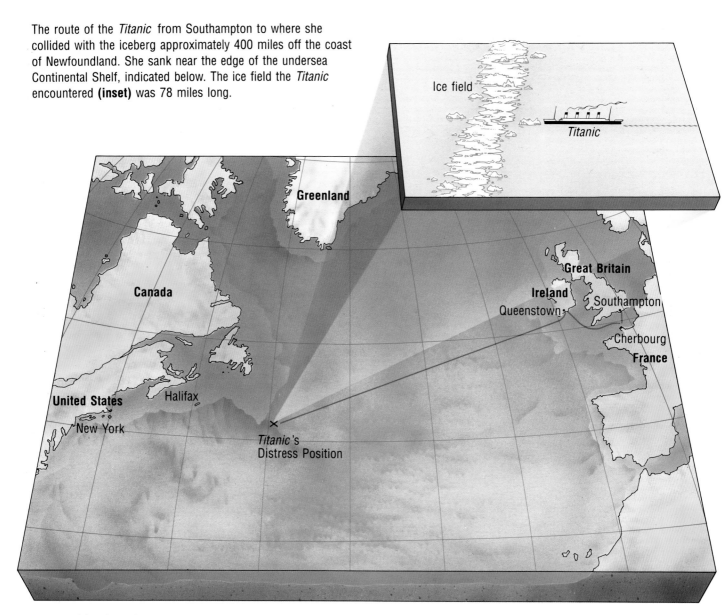

The route of the *Titanic* from Southampton to where she collided with the iceberg approximately 400 miles off the coast of Newfoundland. She sank near the edge of the undersea Continental Shelf, indicated below. The ice field the *Titanic* encountered (**inset**) was 78 miles long.

Ice field

Titanic

Greenland

Canada

Great Britain

Ireland

Queenstown

Southampton

Cherbourg

France

United States

Halifax

New York

✕
Titanic's
Distress Position

Suddenly, Fleet saw something. A huge, dark shape loomed out of the night directly ahead of the *Titanic*. An iceberg! He quickly sounded the alarm bell three times and picked up the telephone.

"What did you see?" asked the duty officer.

"Iceberg right ahead," replied Fleet.

Immediately, the officer on the bridge ordered the wheel turned as far as it would go. The engine room was told to reverse the engines, while a button was pushed to close the doors to the watertight compartments in the bottom of the ship.

The lookouts in the crow's nest braced themselves for a collision. Slowly the ship started to turn. It looked as though they would miss it. But it was too late. They had avoided a head-on crash,

but the iceberg had struck a glancing blow along the *Titanic*'s starboard bow. Several tons of ice fell on the ship's decks as the iceberg brushed along the side of the ship and passed into the night. A few minutes later, the *Titanic* came to a stop.

Many of the passengers didn't know the ship had hit anything. Because it was so cold, almost everyone was inside, and most people had already gone to bed. Ruth Becker and her mother were awakened by the dead silence. They could no longer hear the soothing hum of the vibrating engines from below. Jack Thayer was about to step into bed when he felt himself sway ever so slightly. The engines stopped. He was startled by the sudden quiet.

The iceberg brushing past the *Titanic*. A cross-section of the ship shows how the decks were layered from top to bottom. In the inset picture one can see that the largest part of the iceberg was underwater.

Sensing trouble, Ruth's mother looked out of the door of their second-class cabin and asked a steward what had happened. He told her that nothing was the matter, so Mrs. Becker went back to bed. But as she lay there, she couldn't help feeling that something was very wrong.

Jack heard running feet and voices in the hallway outside his first-class cabin. "I hurried into my heavy overcoat and drew on my slippers. All excited, but not thinking anything serious had oc-

curred, I called in to my father and mother that I was going up on deck to see the fun."

On deck, Jack watched some third-class passengers playing with the ice that had landed on the forward deck as the iceberg had brushed by. Some people were throwing chunks at each other, while a few skidded about playing football with pieces of ice.

Down in the very bottom of the ship, things were very different. When the iceberg had struck, there had been a noise like a big gun going off in one of the boiler rooms. A couple of stokers had been immediately hit by a jet of icy water. The noise and the shock of cold water had sent them running for safety.

(Far left) Captain Edward J. Smith.

(Left) Thomas Andrews, the *Titanic*'s builder.

(Below) A door to one of the *Titanic*'s watertight compartments. These doors could be closed automatically by a switch in the bridge area.

Twenty minutes after the crash, things looked very bad indeed to Captain Smith. He and the ship's builder, Thomas Andrews, had made a rapid tour below decks to inspect the damage. The mail room was filling up with water, and sacks of mail were floating about. Water was also pouring into some of the forward holds and two of the boiler rooms.

Captain Smith knew that the *Titanic*'s hull was divided into a number of watertight compartments. She had been designed so that she could still float if only the first four compartments were flooded, but not any more than that. But water was pouring into the first five compartments. And when the water filled them, it would spill over into the next compartment. One by one all the remaining compartments would flood, and the ship would eventually sink. Andrews told the captain that the ship could last an hour, an hour and a half at the most.

Harold Bride had just awakened in the radio room when Captain Smith stuck his head in the door. "Send the call for assistance," he ordered.

"What call should I send?" Phillips asked.

"The regulation international call for help. Just that." Then the captain was gone. Phillips began to send the Morse code "CQD" distress call, flashing away and joking as he did it. After all, they knew the ship was unsinkable.

Five minutes later, the captain was back. "What are you sending?" he asked.

"CQD," Phillips answered. Then Bride cut in and suggested that they try the new SOS signal that was just coming into use. They began to send out the new international call for help — it was one of the first SOS calls ever sent out from a ship in distress.

Ruth and her family had stayed in their bunks for a good fifteen minutes or so after the room steward had told them nothing was wrong. But Ruth's mother couldn't stop worrying as she heard

At 12:45 a.m. the ship was well down at the bow and the first white distress flares were fired. **(Inset)** The *Titanic* was divided into 16 so-called "watertight" compartments. Because they were not sealed at the top, water from one full compartment could spill over into the next one until the ship eventually sank.

the sound of running feet and shouting voices in the hallway. Poking her head out of the cabin, she found a steward and asked what the matter was.

"Put on your things and come at once," said the steward.

"Do we have time to dress?" she asked.

"No, madam. You have time for nothing. Put on your lifejackets and come up to the top deck."

Ruth helped her mother dress the children quickly. But they only had time to throw their coats over their nightgowns and put on their shoes and stockings. In their rush, they forgot to put on their lifejackets.

Just after midnight, Captain Smith ordered the lifeboats uncovered. The ship's squash court, which was thirty-two feet above the keel, was now completely flooded. Jack Thayer and his father came into the first-class lounge to try to find out exactly what the matter was. When Thomas Andrews, the ship's builder, passed by, Mr. Thayer asked him what was going on. He replied in a low voice that the ship had not much more than an hour to live. Jack and his father couldn't believe their ears.

From the bridge of the *Titanic*, a ship's lights were observed not far away, possibly the *Californian*'s. Captain Smith then ordered white distress rockets fired to get the attention of the nearby ship. They burst high in the air with a loud boom and a shower of stars. But the rockets made no difference. The mystery ship in the distance never answered.

(**Left**) Wives saying goodbye to their husbands as lifeboats are loaded on the Boat Deck.

(**Right**) By 1:40 a.m. the forecastle of the *Titanic* was underwater, and almost all of the lifeboats had been launched.

(**Below**) A crew member in boat No. 13 cuts the lowering ropes just before boat No. 15 comes down on top of them.

In the radio room, Bride and Phillips now knew how serious the accident was, and were feverishly sending out calls for help. A number of ships heard and responded to their calls, but most were too far away to come to the rescue in time. The closest ship they had been able to reach was the *Carpathia*, about fifty-eight miles away. Immediately, the *Carpathia* reported that she was racing full steam to the rescue. But could she get there in time?

Not far away, the radio operator of the *Californian* had gone to bed for the night and turned off his radio. Several officers and crewmen on the deck of the *Californian* saw rockets in the distance and reported them to their captain. The captain told them to try to contact the ship with a Morse lamp. But they received no answer to their flashed calls. No one thought to wake up the radio operator.

On board the *Titanic*, almost an hour after the crash, most of the passengers still did not realize the seriousness of the situation. But Captain Smith was a very worried man. He knew that the *Titanic* only carried lifeboats for barely half the estimated 2,200 people on board. He would have to make sure his officers kept order to avoid any panic among the passengers. At 12:30 a.m. Captain Smith gave the orders to start loading the lifeboats — women and children first. Even though the *Titanic* was by now quite noticeably down at the bow and listing slightly to one side, many passengers still didn't want to leave the huge, brightly lit ship. The ship's band added to a kind of party feeling as the musicians played lively tunes.

About 12:45 a.m., the first lifeboat was lowered. It could carry sixty-five people, but left with only twenty-eight aboard. Indeed, many of the first boats to leave were half empty. Ruth Becker noticed that there was no panic among the crowds

of passengers milling about on the decks. "Everything was calm, everybody was orderly." But the night air was now biting cold. Ruth's mother told her to go back to their cabin to get some blankets. Ruth hurried down to the cabin and came back with several blankets in her arms. The Beckers walked toward one of the lifeboats, and a sailor picked up Ruth's brother and sister and placed them in the boat.

"That's all for this boat," he called out. "Lower away!"

"Please, those are my children!" cried Ruth's mother. "Let me go with them!"

The sailor allowed Mrs. Becker to step into the lifeboat with her two children. She then called back to Ruth to get into another lifeboat. Ruth went to the next boat and asked the officer if she could get in. He said, "Sure," picked her up, and dumped her in.

Boat No. 13 was so crowded that Ruth had to stand up. Foot by foot it was lowered down the steep side of the massive ship. The new pulleys shrieked as the ropes passed through them, creaking under the weight of the boat and its load of sixty-four people. After landing in the water, Ruth's lifeboat began to drift. Suddenly Ruth saw another lifeboat coming down right on top of them! Fear-

ing for their lives, the men in charge of her boat shouted, "Stop!" to the sailors up on the deck. But the noise was so great that nobody noticed. The second lifeboat kept coming down, so close that they could actually touch the bottom of it. All of a sudden, one of the men in Ruth's boat jumped up, pulled out a knife and cut them free of their lowering ropes. Ruth's boat pushed away from the *Titanic* just as boat No. 15 hit the water inches away from them.

Below, in the third-class decks of the ship, there was much more confusion and alarm. Most of these passengers had not yet been able to get above decks. Some of those who did finally make it out had to break down the barriers between third and first class.

By 1:30 a.m. the bow was well down, and people were beginning to notice the slant in the decks. In the radio room, Bride and Phillips were still desperately sending out calls for help: "We are sinking fast...women and children in boats. We cannot last much longer." The radio signal gradually got weaker and weaker as the ship's power faded out. Out on the decks, most passengers now began to move toward the stern area, which was slowly lifting out of the water.

(Next page) The final moments of the *Titanic*.

By 2:05 a.m. there were still over 1,500 people left on the sinking ship. All the lifeboats were now away, and a strange stillness took hold. People stood quietly on the upper decks, bunching together for warmth, trying to keep away from the side of the tilting ship.

Captain Smith now made his way to the radio room and told Harold Bride and Jack Phillips to save themselves. "Men, you have done your full duty," he told them. "You can do no more. Abandon your cabin. Now it's every man for himself." Phillips kept working the radio, hanging on until the very last moment. Suddenly Bride heard water gurgling up the deck outside the radio room. Phillips heard it, too, and cried, "Come on, let's clear out."

Near the stern, Father Thomas Byles had heard confession and given absolution to over one hundred passengers. Playing to the very end, the members of the ship's brave band finally had to put down their instruments and try to save themselves. In desperation, some of the passengers and crew began to jump overboard as the water crept up the slant of the deck.

Jack Thayer stood with his friend Milton Long at the railing to keep away from the crowds. He had become separated from his father in the confusion on deck. Now Jack and his friend heard muffled thuds and explosions deep within the ship. Suddenly the *Titanic* began to slide into the water. The water rushed up at them. Thayer and Long quickly said goodbye and good luck to each other. Then they both jumped.

As he hit the water, Jack Thayer was sucked down. "The cold was terrific. The shock of the water took the breath out of my lungs. Down and down I went, spinning in all directions." When he finally surfaced, gasping for air and numbed by the water, the ship was about forty feet away from him. His friend Milton Long was nowhere to be seen. Jack would never see him again.

Jack Thayer was lucky. As he struggled in the water, his hand came to rest on an overturned lifeboat. He grabbed hold and hung on, barely managing to pull himself up out of the water. Harold Bride had been washed overboard and now also clung to this same boat.

Both Jack and Harold witnessed the mighty ship's last desperate moments. "We could see groups of...people aboard, clinging in clusters or bunches, like swarming bees; only to fall in masses, pairs or singly, as the great part of the ship...rose into the sky..." said Thayer. "I looked upwards — we were right under the three enormous propellers. For an instant, I thought they

Rescue by the *Carpathia*

Captain Arthur Rostron of the *Carpathia* (**inset far right**) is a hero of the *Titanic* story. When his ship received the *Titanic*'s distress call, Captain Rostron immediately gave orders to his crew and raced to the scene through seas made treacherous by icebergs. He arrived at 4:00 a.m. to find only the *Titanic*'s lifeboats and 705 of her passengers and crew. In the photograph (**below**) and illustration (**below, right**) the *Titanic*'s lifeboats approach the *Carpathia* in the early dawn. A crewman pokes his head out (**far right**) to observe *Titanic* passengers preparing to board the *Carpathia*. The overturned lifeboat (**right**) was the one Harold Bride and Jack Thayer clung to throughout the night. It was a canvas-sided lifeboat that had been stowed on the roof of the officers' quarters. When the *Titanic* sank it was washed overboard and provided refuge for 28 people.

were sure to come right down on top of us. Then...she slid quietly away from us into the sea."

Out in the safety of her lifeboat, Ruth Becker also witnessed the end of the *Titanic*. "I could look back and see this ship, and the decks were just lined with people looking over. Finally, as the *Titanic* sank faster, the lights died out. You could just see the stern remaining in an upright position for a couple of minutes. Then...it disappeared."

Then, as Ruth recalled, "there fell upon the ear the most terrible noise that human beings ever listened to — the cries of hundreds of people struggling in the icy cold water, crying for help with a cry we knew could not be answered." In Thayer's

words, they became "a long continuous wailing chant." Before long this ghastly wailing stopped, as the freezing water took its toll.

Jack Thayer and Harold Bride and a number of other survivors clung to their overturned lifeboat, inches away from an icy death in the North Atlantic. Numb from the cold and not daring to move in case the boat sank under their weight, they prayed and waited for help. Then, as the first light of dawn crept on the horizon, a rocket was seen in the distance. The *Carpathia* had come to their rescue.

CHAPTER FOUR

Discovery

"LIFEBOATS!" I SAID EXCITEDLY TO JEAN-LOUIS, pointing at the map on the plotting table. "We know that the *Carpathia* picked up the lifeboats right about here. The *Titanic* must be north of that point. If we start there and work north, we're bound to find her." My French partner and friend Jean-Louis Michel and I huddled over the maps and charts spread out before us. We were aboard the Woods Hole research ship *Knorr*. Out in the middle of the Atlantic Ocean, in August, 1985, we were plotting a new strategy in our search for the *Titanic*. After six weeks, we had found nothing. Now some new thinking was called for. I was also praying that our luck would finally turn.

In the dangerous stretch of the northwest Atlantic where the *Titanic* sank, there are only a few months during the year when the weather is likely to be good. Even then, terrible storms are possible. Now we had barely five weeks to complete our difficult mission. Five weeks not only to find the *Titanic* miles down in the middle of

Jean-Louis Michel and I plot our strategy on board the *Knorr*.

nowhere, but to bring back photographs of the wreck for the waiting world to see. My dream of finding the *Titanic* was turning out to be a constant fight against time and nature.

The expedition I had waited so long for was a joint French-American undertaking. Jean-Louis Michel and I had spent the first six weeks on board the French ship *Le Suroit*. We had used Jean-Louis' brand-new SAR system, a sonar tracking instrument that looked like a red torpedo. But we had not found anything. We had covered a lot of ground, but the ocean currents had been very strong. They had often pushed us off course, wasting precious time. Already we were behind schedule.

Sonar is used to find underwater objects by bouncing electronic sound waves off them. Towing Jean-Louis' SAR sonar "torpedo" underwater just above the ocean floor was a bit like towing a kite on a two-and-a-half-mile string. And it had to be towed carefully back and forth so we wouldn't miss anything. An 882-foot-long ship is only a tiny speck in the vast ocean depths, with its underwater canyons and crevices. Unless we covered every yard of our search area, we might miss our target. We called it "mowing the lawn." Being careful and thorough day after day with no results got to be very tiring, and very boring.

For the first while, the weather had been good. Then storms blew in, and we were bounced around like a cork in a churning whirlpool. This was not only rough and unpleasant; it also meant wasted time as we were forced to stop searching.

Jean-Louis and his crack French team had done their best, but, sadly, after six weeks we still

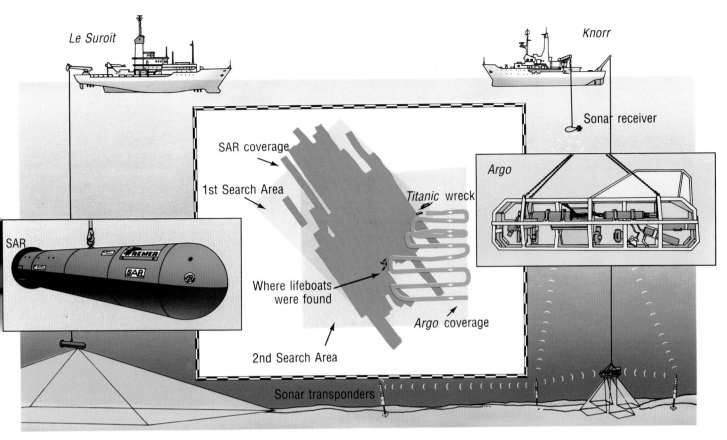

Le Suroit

Knorr

Sonar receiver

SAR coverage

1st Search Area

Titanic wreck

Argo

SAR

Where lifeboats
were found

Argo coverage

2nd Search Area

Sonar transponders

This diagram shows how the two parts of our 1985 expedition worked together to find the *Titanic*. The French ship *Le Suroit* with its SAR sonar vehicle **(left)**, covered 80 percent of the 150-mile target search area. With the American ship *Knorr* and the deep-towed camera sled *Argo* **(right)** we worked north in wide arcs, taking video pictures of the ocean bottom hoping to locate debris from the *Titanic*.

hadn't found any sign of the *Titanic*. It was now up to the American half of the expedition, along with Jean-Louis and two of his team, to try to find our target.

When we moved from *Le Suroit* to the *Knorr*, we also moved from using sonar technology to using video cameras. The *Knorr* was geared to tow one of my pet pieces of equipment, *Argo*. *Argo* is basically a steel sled with video cameras that film the ocean floor. Its moving images are sent up the tow cable to video screens on the ship, so we could see instantly what *Argo* was seeing on the bottom.

As we settled in to the new ship, tension began to mount. We all knew that time was fast running out. To have any chance at all now, we had to push really hard in our hunt for the *Titanic*.

And that's why I decided on a new search plan. I knew that when things fall in deep water, they tend to be scattered by ocean currents. The result is usually a long comet tail of debris that settles on the sea floor. I thought that this must have happened when the *Titanic* sank. A long trail of objects would have scattered out of her as she plunged to the bottom. And because the trail would cover a wider area than the ship itself, it would be easier to find. So to save time and make the search easier, I decided to look for the debris field, instead of the *Titanic*. I also hoped that cameras would succeed where sonar had failed. Starting just south of where the lifeboats were found in 1912, we decided to work north and run *Argo* in east-west lines over the search area.

With our new plan in place, it was time to swing into action. Our search team poured into the control room to man their stations. *Argo* was ready to dive. The smell of hot buttered popcorn filled the room. We were relaxed, but concentrating on the job ahead. After the long slow trip out to the site, we were finally getting down to business.

MAIN BOILERS

(Above) One of the *Titanic*'s boilers lying on the ocean floor.
(Left) This 1912 photograph of boilers being assembled helped us identify the large round object we saw on *Argo*'s video screen.

But as *Argo* reached the ocean bottom at a depth of 12,690 feet from the surface, its cameras revealed only faint tracks of deep-sea slugs etched in the mud. Otherwise, nothing. For the next several days all we saw was a gently rolling countryside made up of hills of mud.

Towing *Argo* was a delicate balancing act. If the *Knorr* went too fast, *Argo* would lift too high off the bottom for its cameras to see anything. If the ship's speed was too slow, *Argo* might crash to the bottom. Keeping a tight balance between *Knorr* and *Argo* was very tough and very tiring work. And it went on hour after hour, day after day.

Then we had only five days left to go. The crunch had come. Suddenly the ocean seemed huge, and our doubts began to grow. Was the *Titanic* really in our carefully plotted search area? If so, surely something would have shown up on our monitor screens by now. Were we looking in the wrong place? Would we return empty-handed? I began to feel a rising panic.

In a last-ditch effort, we decided to check out a tiny portion of ocean bottom that Jean-Louis and his SAR sonar system had missed because of strong currents. We headed to that spot ten miles away.

But as we began to tow *Argo* back and forth across the new search area, our hopes really began to fade. There was nothing down there. By now the routine inside our control room had become mind-numbing: hour after hour of staring at video images of flat bottom mud. On top of that, we were exhausted. The strain of it all was getting to us, and the boredom was becoming unbearable. Then, with a bad turn in the weather and only four days left, we reached our lowest point. I began to face total defeat.

Just after midnight, on September 1, I went to my bunk for some rest, and the night shift led by Jean-Louis manned their stations. About an hour into their watch, one of the team members asked the others, "What are we going to do to keep ourselves awake tonight?" All they'd seen so far was mud and more mud, endless miles of nothing. Stu Harris, who was busy flying *Argo*, didn't answer. His eyes were glued to the *Argo* video monitor.

"There's something," he said, pointing to the screen. Suddenly every member of the sleepy watch was alive and alert. No one could believe it wasn't just another false alarm, or a joke. But, no, there on the screen were clear images of things man-made. Stu yelled, "Bingo!" The control room

A celebration breaks out in the control room after we realize that we have found the *Titanic*.

echoed with a loud "Yeah!" from the whole team, and then wild shrieks and war-whoops. All sorts of wreckage began to stream by on the screen. Then something different appeared — something large and perfectly round. Jean-Louis checked in a book of pictures of the *Titanic*. He came across a picture of the ship's massive boilers, used to burn coal and drive the engines. He couldn't believe his eyes. He looked from book to video screen and back again. Yes, it was the same kind of boiler!

I scrambled out of my bunk when I got the news and ran to the control room. We replayed the tape of the boiler. I didn't know what to say. I turned to Jean-Louis. The look in his eyes said everything. The *Titanic* had been found. We'd been right all along. Then he said softly, "It was not luck. We earned it."

Our hunt was almost over. Somewhere very near us lay the R.M.S. *Titanic*.

Word had spread throughout the ship. People were pouring into the control room. The place was becoming a madhouse. Everyone was shaking hands and hugging and slapping each other on the back.

It was now almost two in the morning, very close to the exact hour of the *Titanic*'s sinking. Someone pointed to the clock on the wall. All of a sudden the room became silent.

Here at the bottom of the ocean lay not only the graveyard of a great ship, but of more than 1,500 people who had gone down with her. And we were the very first people in seventy-three years to come to this spot to pay our respects. Images from the night of the disaster — a story I now knew by heart — flashed through my mind.

Out on the stern of the *Knorr*, people had started to gather for a few moments of silence in memory of those who had died on the *Titanic*. The sky was filled with stars; the sea was calm. We raised the Harland & Wolff flag, the emblem of the shipyard in Belfast, Ireland, that had built the great liner. Except for the shining moon overhead, it was just like the night when the *Titanic* had gone down. I could see her as she slipped nose first into the glassy water. Around me were the ghostly shapes of lifeboats and the piercing shouts and screams of passengers and crew freezing to death in the water.

Our little memorial service lasted about ten minutes. Then I just said, "Thank you all. Now let's get back to work."

In the short time remaining, I planned to get as many pictures of the wreck as possible. I wanted to show the world what condition the *Titanic* was in after seventy-three years on the bottom. A million questions flew through my mind. Would the ship be in one piece or broken up? Were the funnels still standing upright? Would the wooden deck be preserved in the deep salt water? And, a darker thought — would we find any remains of the people who had died that night? Photographs would give us the answers.

We started to make our first run with *Argo* over the major piece of wreckage we'd just found. But there were dangers lurking below. If *Argo* got caught in tangled wreckage, it would take a miracle to free it. It could mean the end of our mission.

As *Argo* neared the bottom, no one moved in the control room. Not a word was spoken. Now *Argo* was passing over the main hull of the *Titanic*. It was time to take a close look.

"Take it down farther. Go down to sixteen feet."

"Roger."

On the video screen, I could see the dim outline of a hull. "It's the side of the ship. She's upright!"

Suddenly, out of the gloom the Boat Deck of the ship came into view. "Keep your eyes peeled for funnels."

But there were only gaping holes where funnels had once stood. Then as we crossed over the middle of the ship, we could see the flattened outline of the bridge. Was this where Captain Smith had stood bravely to the end?

Before we knew it, *Argo* had safely passed over the wreck and back into the empty murk. We had made it safely after all. All at once the crowded control room exploded. People were whooping, hugging, and dancing around while Jean-Louis and I quietly stood there thinking about what we had just seen. We now knew that the *Titanic* had landed on the bottom upright, and that a major piece of her appeared to be intact.

I wanted to make more passes over the wreck with *Argo*, but first it was time to clear the control room. I needed my team as rested as possible for the next sixty-four hours, which was all the time

(Above) Our remote-controlled camera sled, *Argo*, is operated from the control van by a joystick — just like a video game.

(Below) Our two search ships, *Le Suroit* and *Knorr*, are tiny compared to the *Titanic*.

Knorr Le Suroit R.M.S. *Titanic*

we had left. "Hey, we've got too many people up. You'll all be exhausted when your watch comes up. Let's get some of you back in bed. This is a twenty-four hour operation."

During the rest of that afternoon and evening, we managed only two more *Argo* passes over the wreck because of bad weather. But we did discover to our surprise and sadness that the ship was broken in two — her stern was missing. Where the back of the ship should have been, our video images faded into a confusing mass of twisted wreckage.

(Above) We begin the task of lowering *Argo* down to the *Titanic*.

437 ft/133m
This is the deepest a scuba diver has ever gone.

1,500 ft/465 m
Naval submarines dive no deeper than this. There is no light below this level.

3,028 ft/940 m
Pioneer underwater explorers William Beebe and Otis Barton reached this depth in a ball-shaped bathysphere in 1930.

1mile/1,609 m
Many sea creatures here are transparent or can glow in the dark.

2 miles/3,218 m
The water temperature at this depth stays a few degrees above the freezing point.

12,460 ft/3,965 m
The water pressure where the *Titanic* lies is approximately 6,000 lbs per square inch.

Great Pyramid of Cheops El Gizeh, Egypt

Eiffel Tower Paris, France

Empire State Building New York, U.S.A.

Sears Tower Chicago, U.S.A.

Ostankino Tower Moscow, Russia

CN Tower Toronto, Canada

This scale drawing shows the enormous distance between the *Knorr* and the *Titanic* wreck.

By now the storm had reached its peak. We could no longer use *Argo*. For ten hours the wind howled across our rolling deck as the *Knorr* pitched and heaved in the rough sea. Well, I thought finally, if we can't use *Argo* and the video system, then we'll work with ANGUS.

ANGUS was quite like *Argo*, except that it was an older camera sled that took still photographs instead of video as it was towed over the sea floor. Our nickname for ANGUS was the "dope on a rope." Now we would bring our old friend to the rescue. After all, I had used ANGUS in rougher seas than this.

But our first runs over the wreck with ANGUS only produced blurry images. The cameras were working properly, but we had come over the wreck too high to get good pictures. We were now down to our final hours, and I felt victory slipping away. At that moment I just wanted to go home. My leg was sore from a fall on the deck, and I hadn't slept in days. We had found the *Titanic*. Wasn't that good enough? Who said we had to bring home pretty pictures?

But somehow I found the strength to continue. I was not going to leave the *Titanic* without trying one last time. We had four and a half hours left before we had to start back. The *Knorr* had to be back in port for another expedition.

I was so tired that I had to lie down or I would fall down. So I lay down in the control room and gave the commands for the last-ditch attempt. What we were about to do in these rough seas was even crazier than the risky ANGUS passes we had just made. We had to get our cameras within close range of the *Titanic*'s decks. On the surface the seas were heaving up and down at least ten to thirteen feet. That motion would travel down our 12,500 feet of cable and make ANGUS hard to control. But what the heck, it was now or never.

"Down to thirteen feet," I croaked.

"Thirteen feet? Are you crazy?" said the pilot.

"Thirteen feet," I repeated.

For the next three hours hardly a word was spoken as we made pass after hair-raising pass over the *Titanic*. One slip and ANGUS would be lost forever in the wreckage below. Outside, the

(Left) One of the pictures ANGUS took of the *Titanic*'s forecastle deck. Two large windlasses and the anchor chains can be clearly seen. The inset photograph shows how this same deck looked 74 years earlier.

(Right) The crow's nest was still attached to the fallen foremast. The 1912 photograph of the crow's nest (inset) shows the bell that was rung when the iceberg was sighted.

wind rattled the walls of our control room as the storm blew itself out. Then, at about six in the morning, a simple message boomed over the *Knorr*'s intercom from the captain: "You have to start up now."

Right on time, ANGUS was pulled back on deck. A few hours later, news came from our photo lab that we had good, clear photographs of the *Titanic*. We'd made it! By a whisker.

Now, finally, I went to my bunk to get some sleep. When I awoke, it was nighttime, and the good ship *Knorr* was steaming quietly and steadily to our home port.

On the clear, warm morning of September 9, 1985, as we steamed down Nantucket Sound, Massachusetts, the *Knorr* was mobbed by helicopters, small planes, and pleasure craft running circles around us and blowing their horns. News of our discovery of the *Titanic* had made headlines around the world.

Then a small boat with a welcoming party including my wife and two sons, Todd and Douglas, approached our ship. Having my family there was

really important to me. They had paid a big price over the years during my long months away from home, but they'd never once complained.

As we came into port, I couldn't believe my eyes. The dock was a mass of people filling every square inch of space. There was a platform bristling with television cameras and reporters. Banners were flying, a band was playing, schoolchildren hung on to balloons, and a cannon boomed out a salute.

What a victory welcome!

We are greeted by a large crowd on our return home.

CHAPTER FIVE

Exploring the Great Ship

WITH A BIG GRIN, I TURNED AND GAVE THE "thumbs up" sign for good luck to the crew standing on the deck of our new research ship, *Atlantis II*. In stocking feet I began to climb down the ladder inside *Alvin*, our tiny submarine. It was July 13, 1986, almost a year after our French-American expedition had first found the *Titanic* and taken photographs of her. Unfortunately, our French colleagues were not able to join us this year. I would miss my friend Jean-Louis.

We had steamed out to where the *Titanic* lay in the treacherous North Atlantic. Now it was time to take a closer look at her.

Our goal was to dive two and a half miles into the pitch-black freezing depths to where the

I climb into *Alvin* to begin preparing for our descent to the wreck of the *Titanic*.

Titanic lay. Then we would try to land *Alvin* on her decks. If all went well, we would be the first human beings in seventy-four years to see the legendary ship at close range.

We closed *Alvin*'s hatch, and I exchanged glances with my pilot and co-pilot as we felt our submarine gently rocking back and forth. We knew that meant we were now dangling half over the deck of *Atlantis II* and half over the water — one of the most dangerous moments of a dive. Should the sub suddenly fall, we could all get badly hurt.

But we hit the water safely. Then our lift line was released, and divers swarmed over the sub checking everything, including *Jason Junior*, or *JJ*. *JJ* was our remote-controlled underwater robot, who was attached to the outside of *Alvin* in a special garage. He operated on a long cable attached to our sub and was equipped with still and video cameras. With his help we hoped to explore inside the wreck below.

The three of us were crammed into the tiny cabin, our inner space capsule. Hemmed in by panels of instruments, we had no room to stretch out or stand up. We were like three sardines in a spherical can. It was warm and stuffy, but the ice-cold water outside would soon cool *Alvin*'s hull, both outside and inside.

Daylight began to fade into deeper and deeper blues as our sub reached its maximum descent speed of 100 feet per minute. It would take us two and a half hours to reach the bottom. There was little talking as we fell swiftly into utter darkness. Soft music played on the sub's stereo.

Alvin and Jason Junior

1) *Alvin*'s titanium pressure sphere.
2) Manipulator arm with lights and still and video cameras.
3) Forward-looking TV camera.
4) Down-looking TV camera.
5) Viewport.
6) Thruster.
7) *Jason Jr.* in his garage.
8) Tether to *Jason Jr.* from *Alvin*.
9) Still and video cameras.
10) Compass.
11) Strobe light.
12) Light.
13) Docking Rail.

Suddenly, a white-tipped shark appeared outside my window and disappeared just as quickly. Sharks often swim by *Alvin* to investigate the noise. It was comforting to know that two inches of metal protected us. I remembered the time a swordfish had attacked *Alvin* and got its sword stuck in the sub.

The long fall to the bottom is usually a lulling experience. The interior gets darker and darker and begins to cool until, after less than fifteen minutes, the sub has reached a depth of 1,200 feet and total darkness. To conserve power, *Alvin*'s outside lights are left off. The only illumination inside comes from three small red lights.

But this time we had technical problems to worry about. First, we discovered that *Alvin*'s sonar had stopped working. Probably either the cold seawater or the increasing pressure had damaged it. Sonar guided us by bouncing electronic sound waves off anything in our path. Without sonar we couldn't see beyond a few yards. Our surface navigator on board *Atlantis II* would have

to guide us to the *Titanic* with his sonar and our sub-to-ship telephone.

A few minutes later, at about 2,000 feet, we passed through what is known as a deep-scattering layer, because it shows up like a cloudy blur on sonar. In fact, the cloud is made up of thousands and thousands of tiny creatures that live at this depth of the ocean. Many of them glow in the dark, their small bodies exploding like fireworks as they become aware of our presence. When I first saw these creatures, they reminded me of a tiny passenger train with lighted windows passing by at night.

By the time we had passed 5,000 feet, almost one hour into our dive, it was getting cold in the sub. We put on our first layers of extra clothing. I was wearing a wool hat from my sons' hockey team to keep my head warm. During the long hours in the tiny cabin, my legs often fell asleep, and sometimes I'd get a bad cramp in my hip. At times like that, *Alvin*'s cabin was more like a torture chamber than a space capsule.

Ten minutes later, at 6,000 feet, our pilot noticed that the instrument panel was showing a salt-water leak into the battery banks that power the sub. Our time on the bottom of the ocean would have to be awfully short today. And to make things even worse, the surface navigator's sonar suddenly stopped working. That meant we were now almost completely blind.

Inside the *Alvin*'s cramped pressure sphere, pilot Dudley Foster checks the submarine's depth while I talk to the *Atlantis II* on the underwater telephone. On either side of Dudley are two of the *Alvin*'s viewports through which we could peer out at the ocean bottom.

Our lights pierced the blackness as the ocean bottom slowly emerged from the dark-green gloom below us. We'd arrived. The only trouble was, we didn't know where we were. All we could see through the portholes was our own shadow cast by *Alvin*'s lights, and some gently rolling ground covered with mud.

So close and yet so far away. The ship lay somewhere near us, probably no more than 400 feet — the length of two city blocks. But when you're more than two miles down in black murk, a few hundred feet without any guiding sonar might as well be a thousand miles.

I couldn't believe it. I'd waited thirteen long years for this moment, and now, a stone's throw away from my dream, I was trapped inside a sardine can on my hands and knees staring at nothing but mud.

Suddenly, a head-splitting alarm buzzer pierced the silence inside our tiny sub. The leak in our battery was getting to the critical point. We had very little time left if we were to get back to the surface without damaging *Alvin*. Quickly, we decided to guess where the *Titanic* might be and blindly go there in a last-ditch throw of the dice.

Alvin now gently touched the bottom with its single runner, like a one-legged skier, and we began to inch along. The shrill alarm was starting

As we shine *Alvin*'s lights on the hull plates of the *Titanic*, it seems like we have been stopped on the ocean floor by a huge wall of steel.

to drive us crazy, and the tension in the sub was heavy. Our time was running out fast. It was going to be a very close call if we hoped to see the *Titanic*.

Then our surface navigator called in on the telephone with the good news that his sonar was working again, and that "the *Titanic* should be about fifty yards west of us."

We turned the sub and strained our eyes to see out the portholes. Now the bottom began to look strange. It began to slope sharply upward, as though it had been bulldozed into place. My heartbeat quickened.

"Come right," I said to the pilot. "I think I see a wall of black just on the other side of that mud mound."

Then, directly in front of us, there it was: an endless slab of rusted steel rising out of the bottom — the massive hull of the *Titanic*! I felt like a space voyager peering at an alien city wall on some empty planet. Slowly, I let out my breath; I didn't realize I had been holding it.

But one look at the fabulous wreck was all I got. Our pilot quickly dropped *Alvin*'s weights, clicked off that horrible alarm, and we went hurtling toward the surface. One moment longer on the bottom, and *Alvin*'s power system would have been in extreme danger.

All we had to show for six hours' work was a brief glimpse of the *Titanic*. But my dream had finally come true.

(Far left) As *Alvin*'s lights glow from above, *Jason Junior* explores the *Titanic*'s starboard anchor.

(Left) The port anchor as it appeared when the *Titanic* was launched.

(Below) The port anchor today, encrusted with rust.

I was in a grim mood when I stepped out of the sub onto the deck of the *Atlantis II*. "I saw the ship for about ten seconds," I said. "But we've got a sick puppy here, and we've got to fix it." If we wanted to dive the next day, we had to take care of our growing list of technical problems. While I slept, our team of experts worked through the night to cure our sick submarine.

Luckily it was all systems go the next morning, and we were full of confidence as we began a second dive. Our goal was to check out possible landing sites for *Alvin* on the decks of the *Titanic*.

Our second view of the *Titanic* was breathtaking. As we glided soundlessly across the ocean bottom, the razor's edge of the bow loomed out of the darkness. The great ship towered above us. Suddenly it seemed to be coming right at us, about to run us over. My first reaction was that we had to get out of the way. But the *Titanic* wasn't going anywhere. As we gently brought our sub closer,

we could see the bow more clearly. Both of her huge anchors were still in place. But the bow was buried more than sixty feet in mud, far too deep for anyone to pull her out of the ooze.

It looked as though the metal hull was slowly melting away. What seemed like frozen rivers of rust covered the ship's side and spread out over the ocean bottom. It was almost as if the blood of the great ship lay in pools on the ocean floor.

As *Alvin* rose in slow motion up the ghostly side of the ship, I could see our lights reflecting off the still-unbroken glass of the *Titanic*'s portholes. They made me think of cats' eyes gleaming in the dark. In places the rust formations over the portholes looked like eyelashes with tears, as though the *Titanic* were crying. I could also see a lot of reddish-brown stalactites of rust over the wreck, like long icicles. I decided to call them "rusticles." This rust turned out to be very fragile. If touched by our sub, it disappeared like a cloud of smoke.

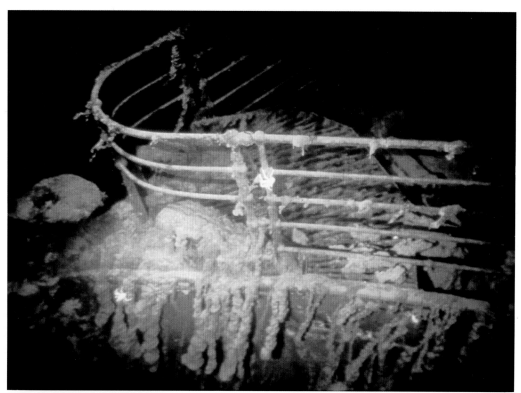

(Right) The curved railing at the front of the bow.

(Below) How the *Titanic*'s bow railing looked 74 years earlier.

(Bottom) Rusticles hang from two large bollards.

As we rose further and began to move across the mighty forward deck, I was amazed at the sheer size of everything: giant bollards and shiny bronze capstans that were used for winding ropes and cables; the huge links of the anchor chains. When you were there on the spot, the ship was truly titanic.

I strained to get a good look at the deck's wood planking, just four feet below us. Then my heart dropped to my stomach. "It's gone!" I muttered. Most of the *Titanic*'s wooden deck had been eaten away. Millions of little wood-eating worms had done more damage than the iceberg and the salt water. I began to wonder whether the

metal deck below the destroyed wood planking would support our weight when *Alvin* landed.

We would soon find out. Slowly we moved into position to make our first landing test on the forward deck just next to the fallen mast. As we made our approach, our hearts beat quickly. We knew there was a real risk of crashing through the deck. The sub settled down, making a muffled crunching noise. If the deck gave way, we'd be trapped in collapsing wreckage. But it held, and we settled firmly. That meant there was a good chance that the *Titanic*'s decks would support us at other landing sites.

We carefully lifted off and turned toward the stern. The dim outline of the ship's superstructure came into view: first B Deck, then A, finally the Boat Deck — the top deck where the bridge was located. It was here that the captain and his officers had guided the ship across the Atlantic. The wooden wheelhouse was gone, probably knocked away in the sinking. But the bronze telemotor control to which the ship's wheel had once been attached stood intact, polished to a shine by the current. We then safely tested this second landing site.

The *Titanic*'s Bridge in 1912

The bridge area was Captain Smith's headquarters for guiding the ship's course. A cutaway reveals the navigation instruments.

1) Telemotor with ship's wheel.
2) Telephone that received the fatal iceberg message from the lookout.
3) Telegraph that sent messages to the engine rooms.
4) Telegraph used while docking.
5) Binnacle or ship's compass.
6) Auxiliary wheel.
7) Bridge wing and cab.
8) Forward funnel.
9) Forward davit for lifeboat No. 2.
10) Cargo cranes.
11) Cargo hatch No. 3.
12) Officers' quarters.
13) Whistles.

The *Titanic*'s Bridge in 1986

With its wheelhouse washed away and the foremast lying across it, the bridge is a changed scene today.

1) Telemotor without wheel.
2) Remains of base of wheelhouse.
3) Fallen foremast.
4) Mast light.
5) Dislodged lifeboat davits.
6) First-class state-rooms.
7) Collapsed bridge cab.
8) Hole where forward funnel stood.
9) No. 2 lifeboat davit.
10) Cargo cranes.
11) Cargo hatch No. 3.

The wooden ship's wheel **(far left)** has disappeared but its bronze telemotor control **(left)** still stands on the bridge.

Jason Junior illuminates a pillar still standing in the foyer of the Grand Staircase. *Alvin* has landed on the Boat Deck beside the collapsed roof that once held the glass dome over the staircase. From inside the submarine we guide *JJ* down the staircase shaft as far as B Deck.

I had an eerie feeling as we glided along exploring the wreck. As I peered through my porthole, I could easily imagine people walking along the deck and looking out the windows of the ship that I was looking into. Here I was at the bottom of the ocean looking at a kind of time capsule from history.

Suddenly, as we rose up the port side of the ship, the sub shuddered and made a clanging noise. A waterfall of rust covered our portholes. "We've hit something!" I exclaimed. "What is it?"

"I don't know," our pilot replied. "I'm backing off." Unseen overhangs are the nightmare of the deep-sub pilot. Carefully, the pilot backed away from the hull and brought us slowly upward. Then, directly in front of our forward porthole, a big lifeboat davit slid by. We had hit one of the metal arms that held the lifeboats as they were lowered. This davit was one of the two that had held boat No. 8, the boat Mrs. Straus had refused to enter that night. She was the wife of the owner of Macy's department store in New York. When she had been offered a chance to save herself in one of the lifeboats, she had turned to her husband and said, "We have been living together for many years. Where you go, I go." Calmly, the two of them had sat down on a pile of deck chairs to wait for the end.

Now, as we peered out our portholes, it seemed as if the Boat Deck were crowded with passengers. I could almost hear the cry, "Women and children first!"

We knew from the previous year's pictures that the stern had broken off the ship, so we continued back to search for the severed end of the intact bow section. Just beyond the gaping hole where the second funnel had been, the deck be-

(**Above**) The Grand Staircase in 1912. The ornate clock from the landing is now only a scar on the wall behind the loop in *JJ* 's tether (**opposite**). Traces of the staircase's former elegance can be seen in the light fixture (**top left**) from which a piece of coral has sprouted and in the base of one of the oak pillars (**middle left**). How they looked 74 years earlier is indicated in the photograph (**above**). The illustration (**bottom left**) shows a cross-section of *JJ* 's descent with an outline of the original staircase.

gan to plunge down at a dangerous angle. The graceful lines of the ship disappeared in a twisted mess of torn steel plating, upturned portholes, and jumbled wreckage. We saw enough to know that the decks of the ship had collapsed in on one another like a giant accordion. With an unexpectedly strong current pushing us toward this twisted wreckage, we veered away and headed for the surface.

The next day we landed on the deck next to the very edge of the Grand Staircase, which had once been covered by an elegant glass dome. The dome hadn't survived the plunge, but the staircase shaft had, and to me it still represented the fabulous luxury of the ship. *Alvin* now rested quietly on the top deck of the R.M.S. *Titanic* directly above the place where three elevators had carried first-class passengers who did not wish to use the splendid Grand Staircase.

We, however, would take the stairs with *JJ* the robot, our R2D2 of the deep. This would be

the first deep-water test for our remote-controlled swimming eyeball, and we were very nervous about it. No one knew whether *JJ* 's motors could stand up to the enormous ocean pressure of more than 6,000 pounds per square inch.

Using a control box with a joystick that operated like a video game, the operator cautiously steered *JJ* out of his garage attached to the front of *Alvin.* Slowly *JJ* went inching down into the yawning blackness of the Grand Staircase. More and more cable was let out as he dropped deeper and deeper.

(Left) The ghostly open window of a first-class stateroom.

(Top) *JJ* tries to go in for a closer look.

(Above) A window from Captain Smith's quarters.

We could see what *JJ* was seeing on our video in the sub. But at first *JJ* could see nothing. Then, as he dropped deeper, a room appeared off the portside foyer on A Deck. *JJ* swung around and our co-pilot saw something in the distance. "Look at that," he said softly. "Look at that chandelier."

Now I could see it, too. "No, it can't be a chandelier," I said. "It couldn't possibly have survived."

I couldn't believe my eyes. The ship had fallen two and a half miles, hitting the bottom with the force of a train running into a mountain, and here was an almost perfectly preserved light fixture! *JJ* left the stairwell and started to enter the room, managing to get within a foot of the fixture. To our astonishment, we saw a feathery piece of coral sprouting from it. We could even see the sockets where the light bulbs had been fitted! "This is fantastic," I exulted.

"Bob, we're running short of time. We have to return to the surface." Our pilot's words cut like a knife through my excitement. Here we were deep inside the *Titanic*, actually going down the Grand Staircase, but we had used up all the time that we had to stay safely on the bottom. I knew our pilot was just following orders, but I still wanted to shout in protest.

Our little robot soldier emerged from the black hole and shone his lights toward us, bathing the interior of the sub in an unearthly glow. For a moment it felt as if an alien spaceship were hovering nearby. But that feeling quickly gave way to one of victory, thanks to our little friend. *JJ* had been a complete success.

On our next day's dive, we crossed over what had once been Captain Smith's cabin. Its outer wall now lay collapsed on the deck, as though a giant had brought his fist down on it. We passed within inches of one of the cabin's windows. Was this, I wondered, a window that Captain Smith had cranked open to let a little fresh air into his cabin before going to bed?

Suddenly a large piece of broken railing loomed out of the darkness. It seemed to be heading right for my viewport. I immediately warned

(Above) *JJ* looks in one of the gymnasium windows. (Inset) The gymnasium in 1912. (Top right) The mechanical horse was one of the gym's exercise machines. (Bottom right) The lever that operated the mechanical horse still stands upright.

the pilot who quickly turned *Alvin*'s stern around, rotating us free of the obstacle.

Now we began to drop onto the starboard Boat Deck. As we glided along, I felt as though I were visiting a ghost town where suddenly one day everyone had closed up shop and left.

An empty lifeboat davit stood nearby. Ahead I could see where the *Titanic*'s lifeboats had rested. It was on this very deck that the crowds of passengers had stood waiting to get into the boats. They had not known until the last moments that there were not enough lifeboats for everyone. It was also from this deck that you could have heard the *Titanic*'s brave band playing cheerful music to boost the crowd's spirits as the slope of the deck grew steeper and steeper.

Jason Jr. now went for a stroll along the Boat Deck. As he slowly made his way along, he looked

in the windows of several first-class cabins as well as into some passageways, including one that still bore the words, "First-Class Entrance." As *JJ* passed by the gymnasium windows, I could see bits and pieces of equipment amid the rubble, including some metal grillwork that had been part of the electric camel, an old-fashioned exercise machine. We could also see various wheel shapes and a control lever. Much of the gym's ceiling was covered with rust. This was where the gym instructor, dressed in white flannel trousers, had urged passengers to try the gym machines. And, on the last night, passengers had gathered here for warmth as the lifeboats were being lowered.

I could see *JJ* far off down the deck, turning this way and that to get a better view inside doorways and various windows. It was almost as though our little robot had a mind of his own.

But now we had to bring him home. We had been on the *Titanic* for hours. Once again it was time to head back to the surface.

The Bow Section of the *Titanic*

1) The curved edge of the open A-Deck forward promenade.
2) Rusticles hang from the windows of the enclosed A-Deck promenade.
3) This winch was used only once to raise the lifeboats after a test launch in port.
4) A rusticle hangs over the glass of a C-Deck porthole.

5) Anchor chains went around this windlass.
6) *JJ* examines a bollard on the Forecastle Deck.
7) The arm of a lifeboat davit with its block and pulley still attached. Other similar davit arms are indicated on the painting.
8) Rusticles adorn the prow of the *Titanic*.

9) The anchor crane.
10) Anchor chains on the forecastle.
11) The starboard anchor.
12) The crow's nest on the fallen foremast.
13) Cranes that lowered cargo into the holds.
14) A closed gate between third- and first-class areas.

15) The telemotor that once held the ship's wheel.
16) The collapsed roof of the Grand Staircase.
17) The gymnasium.
18) An opened joint in the ship's structure.
19) A lifeboat davit missing its arm.
20) Hull plates possibly damaged by the iceberg.

The Debris Field

Between the separated sections of the *Titanic* lie thousands of objects that spilled out of the ship when she sank.

The cast-iron frame of one of the benches from the *Titanic*'s decks.

Stern Section

A painted metal footboard from a bed similar to the one shown with Jack Thayer on page 17.

A tin cup and two doorknobs sit by the round furnace door of a rusted boiler.

The morning of July 18 was lovely and warm, but I felt edgy about the day's mission. We had decided to visit the *Titanic*'s debris field. Along the 1,970 feet that separated the broken-off bow and stern pieces of the wreck, there was a large scattering of all kinds of objects from the ship.

Everything from lumps of coal to wrought-iron deck benches had fallen to the bottom as she broke in two and sank. But I was anxious about what we might find down there among the rubble. I had often been asked about the possibility of finding human bodies. It was a chilling thought.

This sink matches the ones pictured with Ruth Becker on page 16.

Bow Section

The white porcelain of this bathtub is almost hidden by rust in contrast **(inset)** to the way it appeared when new.

(Above) This statuette of a Greek goddess once stood on the fireplace in the *Titanic*'s elegant first-class lounge.
We photographed her lying on the ocean floor beside some large stones dropped by melting icebergs.

We had not seen any signs of human remains so far, but I knew that if we were to find any, it would most likely be during this dive.

As the first fragments of wreckage began to appear on the bottom, I felt like we were entering a bombed-out museum. Thousands upon thousands of objects littered the rolling fields of ocean bottom, many of them perfectly preserved. The guts of the *Titanic* lay spilled out across the ocean floor. Cups and saucers, silver serving trays, pots and pans, wine bottles, boots, chamber pots, space heaters, bathtubs, suitcases, and more.

Undersea creatures devoured all but the porcelain head **(right)** of this doll found in the *Titanic*'s debris field. It was an expensive French lady doll like the one shown **(inset)**, and most likely belonged to a first-class passenger. It may have belonged to three-year-old Loraine Allison of Montreal. She was the only child from first class who did not survive the sinking. Loraine is shown **(above)** with her baby brother.

Then, without warning, I found myself looking into the ghostly eyes of a small, white smiling face. For a split second I thought it was a skull — and it really scared me. Then I realized I was looking at a doll's head, its hair and clothes gone.

My shock turned to sadness as I began to wonder who had owned this toy. Had the girl survived in one of the lifeboats? Or had she clutched the doll tightly as she sank in the icy waters?

We moved on through this amazing scenery. There were so many things scattered about that it became difficult to keep track of them. We came across one of the ship's boilers, and there on top of it sat an upright rusty metal cup like the ones the crew had used. It looked as though it had been placed there by a stoker moments before water had burst into the boiler room. It was astonishing

to think that in fact this cup had just fluttered down that night to land right on top of a boiler.

Then in the light of *Alvin*'s headlights, we spotted a safe ahead of us. I had heard about the story of fabulous treasure, including a leather-bound book covered with jewels, being locked in the ship's safes when she sank. Here was the chance of a lifetime, and I wanted to get a good look at it.

The safe sat there with its door face up. The handle looked as though it was made of gold, although I knew it had to be brass. Next to it, I could see a small circular gold dial, and above both a nice shiny gold crest.

Why not try to open it? I watched as *Alvin*'s sample-gathering arm locked its metal fingers onto the handle. Its metal wrist began to rotate clock-

The dial and brass crest of this safe are still shiny. We turned the handle **(left)** with *Alvin*'s mechanical arm. A leather-bound book studded with over 1,000 precious stones **(top left)** may have been placed in one of the *Titanic*'s safes.

wise. To my surprise, the handle turned easily. Then it stopped. The door just wouldn't budge. It was rusted shut. I felt as if I'd been caught with my hand in the cookie jar. Oh, well, I thought, it was probably empty, anyway. In fact, when we later looked at the video footage we had taken, we could see that the bottom of the safe had rusted out. Any treasure should have been spread around nearby, but there was none to be seen. Fortunately, my promise to myself not to bring back anything from the *Titanic* was not put to the test.

Two days passed before I went down to the *Titanic* again. After the rest, I was raring to go at it once more. This time we were going to explore the torn-off stern section that lay 1,970 feet away from the bow. It had been very badly damaged during the plunge to the bottom. Now it lay almost unrecognizable amidst badly twisted pieces of wreckage. We planned to land *Alvin* on the bottom directly behind the stern section and then send *JJ* in under the overhanging hull. Unless the *Titanic*'s three huge propellers had fallen off when she sank, I figured they still ought to be there, along with her enormous 101-ton rudder.

We made a soft landing on the bottom, and discovered that one of *JJ*'s motors wouldn't work. Our dive looked like a washout. I sat glumly staring out of my viewport at the muddy bottom.

Suddenly the mud started to move! Our pilot was slowly inching *Alvin* forward on its single ski right under the dangerous overhanging stern area. He was taking the sub itself to search for the huge propellers. Was he crazy? What if a piece of wreckage came crashing down? But our pilot was a professional, so I figured he must know exactly what he was doing.

I could see an area ahead covered with rusticles that had fallen from the rim of the stern above.

Until now we had had ocean above us. Crossing this point was like taking a dangerous dare. Once on the other side, there was no sure way of escaping if disaster struck. None of us spoke. The only sound in the sub was our breathing.

Slowly a massive black surface of steel plating seemed to inch down toward us overhead. The hull seemed to be coming at us from all sides. As we looked closely, we could see that like the bow, the stern section was buried deep in the mud—

In *Alvin* we explore under the overhanging deck of the *Titanic*'s severed stern section and photograph the buried rudder **(top)**. The badly damaged stern section looks sadly different from the way it looked on sailing day **(above)**.

The plaque we placed on the stern in memory of those who died on the *Titanic*.

forty-five feet or so. Both the middle and the starboard propellers were under the mud. Only about sixteen feet of the massive rudder could be seen rising out of the ooze.

"Let's get out of here," I said. Ever so gently, *Alvin* retraced the path left by its ski. As we crossed over from the area covered with rusticles into the clear, we sighed with relief. We were out of danger. All of us were glad that this adventure was over.

Before we left the bottom this time, however, there was one mission that I wanted to complete. I wanted to place a memorial plaque on the twisted and tangled wreckage of the stern, in memory of all those lost on the *Titanic*. Those who had died had gathered on the stern as the ship had tilted bow first. This had been their final haven. So we rose up the wall of steel to the top of the stern. With great care, *Alvin*'s mechanical arm plucked the plaque from where it had been strapped outside the sub, and gently released it. We watched as it sank quietly to the deck of the stern.

As we lifted off and began our climb to the surface, our camera kept the plaque in view as long as possible. As we rose, it grew smaller and smaller, until finally it was swallowed in the gloom.

We made two more trips down to the *Titanic*. At the end of the final dive, I knew I had visited the great ship for the last time. Two and a half hours later when we reached the surface, everybody on the *Atlantis II* prepared to head for home. Later that night there would be a party on board, but through it all I was still thinking about the *Titanic*: of the people who built her, sailed on her, and died when she went down.

CHAPTER SIX

Solving the Mysteries

WHEN WE RETURNED HOME AFTER OUR 1986 EXpedition, our work had just begun. Now we had to look through the thousands of photographs and the hours and hours of videotape we had taken on the bottom. We wanted to see if we could shed any new light on the story of the *Titanic*. Perhaps we could help solve some of the mysteries that still surround this legendary ship.

We'll probably never know for sure exactly what the iceberg did to the starboard bow of the *Titanic*. Too much of it is buried too deep in mud for anyone to see. But we did learn that some of the steel plates that covered the side of the ship had been knocked apart at their seams. It's likely that the iceberg made few holes in the ship's side, or none at all. Instead, it appears that the force of the iceberg banging against the ship made the steel plates burst apart, letting water rush in through the cracks. But whatever the exact nature of her ice wound, it was enough to sink the ship.

Before we found the *Titanic*, most people thought that she had sunk in one piece. However, there were many eyewitnesses, including Jack Thayer, who reported that the ship had in fact broken in two, the bow plunging down while the stern righted itself for a moment before turning almost on end and then sinking a minute later. Since we found the *Titanic* sitting in two big pieces 1,970 feet apart and pointing in different directions, it does seem almost certain that the ship broke apart at or near the surface.

As the bow sank and the stern rose higher and higher out of the water, the stress on the hull became so great that the ship finally snapped, right between the third and fourth funnels. Eyewitnesses in the *Titanic*'s lifeboats watched in horror. In the words of one survivor, the bow broke off "with a sound like thunder," and soon began its plunge. It was closely followed by various pieces of the ship that crashed into the ocean as the hull and superstructure pulled apart. The heavier these pieces were, the more quickly they sank.

The bow probably hit the bottom before the stern piece, its tremendous force driving it into the ocean floor. A few minutes later, the stern hit bottom even harder, also sinking deep into the mud. For the next several hours, bits and pieces from the ship scattered down to the ocean floor. These were the things we found lying in the debris field.

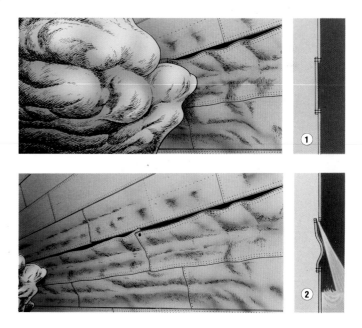

The iceberg scraping against the hull plates of the *Titanic* **(top)** popped many of the steel rivets that held them in place **(top right)**. This allowed water to pour in through the seams **(above right)**.

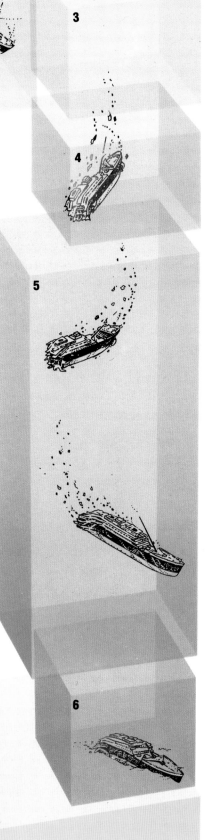

How the *Titanic* Sank

1) At approximately 2:17 a.m. as flooding fills its forward compartments, the *Titanic* lurches downwards and the Number 1 funnel collapses.

2) The ship cannot bear the stress of having its stern in the air and breaks in two between the third and fourth funnels.

3) After the bow section has broken away, the stern section swings around. It remains perpendicular for a few moments before disappearing from sight.

4) As the stern section sinks, much debris falls out and the Poop Deck is peeled over backwards.

5) The stern section falls more or less straight down as the bow section planes off downwards below.

6) The two pieces of the ship land 1,970 feet apart, facing in different directions.

7) The stern slams into the bottom with great force. For several hours afterwards, debris continues to drift down and settle around the wreck.

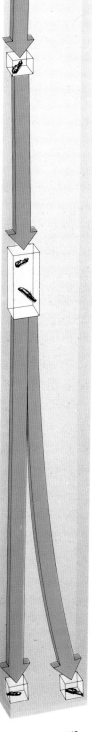

A scale diagram of the descent of the wreck.

We ponder some of the mysteries of the *Titanic* as we return home on the *Atlantis II.*

The ocean is a quiet and fairly stable place. After the *Titanic*'s dramatic final plunge, she lay at a depth of 12,460 feet, where changes happen over tens of years rather than days. First to disappear would have been any soft organic material such as food, then human bodies, the flesh and bones rapidly devoured by fish and crustaceans. Any bones they missed would have been slowly dissolved by the salt water. Clothing would also have gradually vanished over the years.

While we did not find any human remains on our dives, we did discover some chilling evidence. As we were studying our ANGUS pictures, a disturbing image appeared: two matching shoes lying side by side. It was quite clear that they had not landed there by accident. It was as if some invisible person were still wearing them. Before long, another pair of shoes appeared on our ANGUS footage, lying on the bottom in the same way as the first pair. And then we saw yet another pair. There was no doubt about it — we were looking down on the graves of these poor victims, their bodies long gone.

I had hoped that any new expeditions that visited the wreck of the *Titanic* would leave it in peace as we did. To my great disappointment, a French group backed by Swiss and American investors went down to the wreck during the summer of 1987 to gather artifacts from the debris field and bring them up to the surface. In my opinion, this was done purely for profit and shows a great disrespect for the grave site of the victims of the disaster. As survivor Eva Hart said to me, "I'm violently opposed to it. For anyone to go down there and take things is an act of piracy. Those plates they brought up could have been the ones my father ate his last meal from." It is small comfort to know that at least no profit will be made from selling these artifacts in the United States. A resolution has been introduced in the U.S. Congress banning anyone from making a profit with *Titanic* memorabilia in the United States. Congress has already passed legislation calling for the wreck to be made into an international memorial and left undisturbed.

My own treasure from the *Titanic* is in my mind's eye. The first view of the *Titanic* on our second dive will stay with me forever: the huge black shape of the bow looming out of the darkness. Altogether, I visited the *Titanic* nine times, and I got to know her very well. As we landed on her decks and went inside her ravaged interior, I relived the famous scenes from the 1912 tragedy in the actual spots where they had taken place. After each dive, I would come back amazed at what I had seen.

The loss of the *Titanic* was as saddening to the people of that time as the assassination of President John F. Kennedy was to a later time. Something seemed lost forever. People's view of the world is shaken up because of such tragedies. The most recent example is the loss of the space shuttle *Challenger.* As with the *Titanic*, too much confidence was placed in technology. In both cases, the power of nature was overlooked. It seems that we still have something to learn from the *Titanic.*

The *Titanic* is truly gone for good. For that I'm sad, but content. The bottom of the ocean is a peaceful place. In future, when I think of the *Titanic*, I will see her bow sitting upright on the bottom, finally at rest.

EPILOGUE

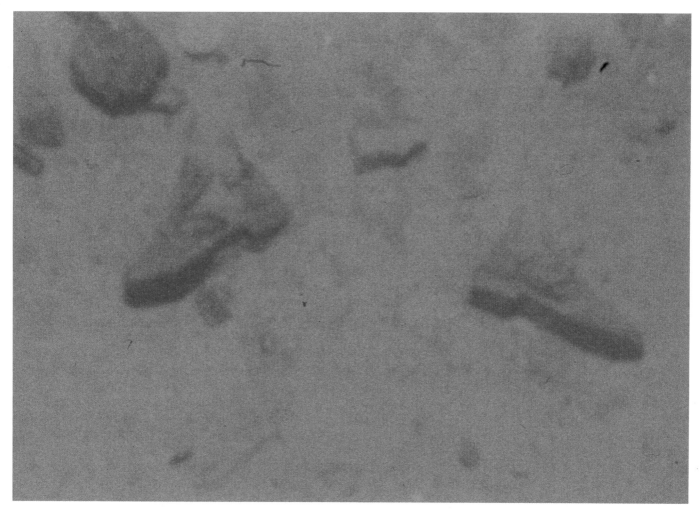

Matching pairs of shoes where bodies once lay remind us that the *Titanic* is a gravesite.

RUTH BECKER WAS REUNITED WITH HER MOTHER, sister, and brother on the *Carpathia*. Her family later moved to the United States, where Ruth eventually married, raised three children, and taught school. Today she is retired and lives in Santa Barbara, California.

Jack Thayer saw his mother as soon he reached the top of the ladder to the deck of the *Carpathia*. She was overjoyed to see him, but sad to discover that her husband had not survived. Jack later wrote a book about his experiences called *The Sinking of the S.S. Titanic.*

Harold Bride collapsed when he reached the deck of the *Carpathia*. He soon recovered and, despite badly frozen feet, spent most of the trip to New York helping the *Carpathia's* radio operator send out news of the disaster.

Jack Phillips, Milton Long, Captain Smith, and more than 1,500 others did not survive.

GLOSSARY

ANGUS: A sled made of steel tubing carrying still cameras. The sled is towed from a ship at the end of a long steel cable. It takes photographs of the ocean floor. The letters in its name stand for Acoustically Navigated Geological Underwater Survey.

Argo: A steel sled equipped with video cameras that take moving television pictures. The pictures are transmitted via the sled's towing cable to the surface, as *Argo* is pulled 60 to 100 feet above the ocean floor.

black smokers: Vents in the ocean floor that belch hot mineral-rich fluids from newly formed volcanic terrain. The temperature of the fluids can reach 800°F (400°C).

Boat Deck: The deck of a ship on which the lifeboats are carried. In the case of the *Titanic*, this was the top deck.

boiler: A furnace in which coal was burned to boil water and create steam, which in turn drove the ship.

bollards: The stout metal posts on a ship or dock to which mooring lines are tied.

bow: The front end of a ship.

bridge: A raised (and usually enclosed) platform or structure toward the front end of a ship, which has a clear view ahead, and from which the ship is navigated.

capstan: An upright, revolving barrel or drum mounted at the bow and stern of a ship. When the ship is at the dock, ropes or cables are wound around it.

CQD: A Morse code distress call used by ships at sea in the early years of the wireless telegraph.

crow's nest: A partly enclosed lookout platform high on a ship's mast.

davits: Crane-like arms on board ship used for holding and lowering lifeboats.

debris field: The area between the separated bow and stern sections of the *Titanic* where many objects from the ship were found.

forward: Toward the front part of a ship.

hold: A storage space for cargo on a ship, usually below decks.

hull: The frame or body of a ship without its superstructure.

hull plates: Metal plates joined together and covering a ship's hull framing. On the *Titanic* they were generally about one inch thick.

Jason Junior (***JJ***): A self-propelled underwater robot equipped with lights and cameras that can explore difficult and dangerous areas. *JJ* was attached to the mini-submarine *Alvin* by a tether and was used to explore the *Titanic*.

keel: A steel line of plates running lengthwise along the middle of the bottom of a ship. It is the "spine" on which the framework of the ship is built.

marine geology: The study of the formation and history of the earth under the seas.

midship: The middle part of a ship.

Morse code: A system invented by Samuel Morse made up of dots and dashes for each letter of the alphabet. Messages can be sent either by radio or by flashing lamp.

Morse lamp: A lamp used to flash signals in Morse code.

plates: Smooth, flat pieces of metal that are hammered together with rivets to cover the frame of a ship.

port: The left-hand side of a ship when facing forward.

rivets: Pins or bolts of steel that hold metal plates together.

R.M.S.: Letters that stand for Royal Mail Steamer.

rusticles: Very fragile reddish-brown stalactites of rust, hanging down as much as several feet, caused by iron-eating bacteria. These rust features cover much of the wreck of the *Titanic*.

SAR: Letters that stand for the French sonar system, Sonar Acoustique Remorqué. It can take the equivalent of visual pictures by bouncing sound waves off objects underwater.

sonar: A system used to detect and locate underwater objects by reflected sound waves.

SOS: A general call for help used by a ship's radio operators when sending Morse code. The letters do *not* stand for "Save Our Ship." The signal was chosen simply because it could be sent and recognized easily in Morse code: 3 dots; 3 dashes; 3 dots.

starboard: The right-hand side of a ship when facing the bow.

stern: The rear end of a ship.

steward: A member of a ship's crew who attends to the needs of passengers and to the food supplies.

stoker: A crew member who keeps a ship's boilers fired to drive the engines.

tidal pools: Pools of water created in rocks along the shoreline by the rising and falling ocean tides.

titanium: A silvery gray, light, and very strong metal.

tube worms: Large worms that live in long white tubes around hydrothermal vents.

wheelhouse: The small covered area on the bridge of a ship where the ship's wheel is located.

wireless: An early form of radio.

A *TITANIC* TIME-LINE

1907

Plans are made to build two huge luxury ships, the *Olympic* and the *Titanic*, with a third, the *Britannic*, to be built later.

1908–1909

Construction of the *Olympic* and the *Titanic* begins in Belfast, Ireland.

1910

OCTOBER 20: The *Olympic* is successfully launched.

1911

MAY 31: The hull of the *Titanic* is successfully launched.

JUNE: The *Olympic* leaves on her maiden voyage.

1912

JANUARY: Sixteen wooden lifeboats, along with four collapsible canvas-sided boats, are fitted on board the *Titanic*.

MARCH 31: The outfitting of the *Titanic* is complete.

APRIL 10: Wednesday — Sailing Day:

9:30 to 11:30 a.m.: Passengers arrive in Southampton and board ship.

Noon: The *Titanic* casts off and begins her maiden voyage.

6:30 p.m.: The *Titanic* rides at anchor in Cherbourg, France.

8:10 p.m.: The *Titanic* leaves for Queenstown, Ireland.

APRIL 11, Thursday: 1:30 p.m.: The *Titanic* leaves Queenstown for New York.

APRIL 12 AND 13, Friday and Saturday: The *Titanic* sails through calm, clear weather.

APRIL 14, Sunday: Seven ice warnings are received during the day.

11:40 p.m.: The lookouts see an iceberg dead ahead. The iceberg strikes the *Titanic* on the starboard (right) side of her bow.

11:50 p.m.: Water has poured in and risen 14 feet in the front part of the ship.

APRIL 15, Monday, 12:00 a.m.: The captain is told that the ship can only stay afloat for a couple of hours. He gives the order to call for help over the radio.

12:05 a.m.: Orders are given to uncover the lifeboats and to get passengers and crew ready on deck. But there is only enough room in the lifeboats for about half of the estimated 2,227 on board.

12:25 a.m.: The order is given to start loading the lifeboats with women and children first. The *Carpathia*, southeast of the *Titanic* by about 58 miles, picks up the distress call and immediately heads full speed to the rescue.

12:45 a.m.: The first lifeboat is safely lowered away. It can carry 65 people, but leaves with only 28 aboard. The first distress rocket is fired. Eight rockets will be fired during the night.

1:15 a.m.: The tilt of the deck grows steeper. Lifeboats now begin to leave more fully loaded.

1:40 a.m.: Most of the forward lifeboats have now gone. Passengers begin to move back to the stern area.

2:05 a.m.: The last lifeboat leaves. There are now over 1,500 people left on the sinking ship. The tilt of the *Titanic*'s decks grows steeper and steeper.

2:17 a.m.: The last radio call for help is sent out. Captain Smith tells crew members, "It's every man for himself." The *Titanic*'s bow plunges under. Many passengers and crew jump overboard. The *Titanic*'s forward funnel collapses, crushing a number of people.

2:18 a.m.: The ship's lights blink once and then go out. Several survivors see the ship break in two. The bow section sinks.

2:20 a.m.: The *Titanic*'s broken-off stern section settles back into the water, becoming more level for a few moments. Slowly it fills with water and again tilts its end high into the air before sinking into the sea. Those struggling in the icy water slowly freeze to death.

3:30 a.m.: The rescue ship *Carpathia*'s rockets are sighted by survivors in the lifeboats.

4:10 a.m.: The first lifeboat is picked up by the *Carpathia*.

8:50 a.m.: The *Carpathia* leaves the area bound for New York. She carries 705 survivors.

APRIL 18, 9:00 p.m.: The *Carpathia* arrives in New York.

APRIL 19 TO MAY 25: An inquiry into the *Titanic* disaster is conducted by the United States Senate.

APRIL 22 TO MAY 15: Several ships are sent to the disaster site to recover bodies. A total of 328 bodies are found floating in the area.

MAY 2 TO JULY 3: The British Inquiry is conducted.

1913

APRIL: As a result of the *Titanic* disaster, the International Ice Patrol is created to guard the North Atlantic sea lanes.

1914

FEBRUARY: The *Titanic*'s second sister ship, the *Britannic*, is launched. She is sunk two years later during World War I.

1935

After 24 years of safe and reliable service, the *Titanic*'s first sister ship, the *Olympic*, is retired and scrapped.

1985

SEPTEMBER 1: A joint French-American scientific expedition led by Dr. Robert Ballard discovers the wreck of the *Titanic*.

1986

JULY: Dr. Ballard returns to the *Titanic*. In a submarine he explores and photographs the entire wreck.

1987

The U.S. Congress moves to make the *Titanic* an international memorial. A French expedition recovers many artifacts from the *Titanic* wreck.

RECOMMENDED FURTHER READING

The Discovery of the Titanic
by Robert D. Ballard 1987
(Warner, U.S. / Hodder and Stoughton, U.K.)
An in-depth account of Robert Ballard's two *Titanic*
expeditions with many photographs.

A Night to Remember
by Walter Lord 1955 (Bantam Books)
The fascinating step-by-step story of what happened the
night the *Titanic* sank.

The Night Lives On
by Walter Lord 1986 (W. Morrow and Co.)
More answers to many of the mysteries about the
Titanic.

The Story of the Titanic
edited by Jack Winocour 1960 (Dover Inc.)
Descriptions by four survivors, including Harold Bride,
of their experiences on the *Titanic.*

The Titanic: End of a Dream
by Wyn Craig Wade 1979 (Penguin Books)
The story of the ship and the U.S. Inquiry.

Titanic: Triumph and Tragedy
by John P. Eaton and Charles A. Haas 1986
(Norton, U.S. / Patrick Stephens, U.K.)
A detailed reference book with hundreds of photographs of the ship, her passengers, and crew.

PICTURE CREDITS

Front Cover: (Top) Painting by Ken Marschall (Left) Perry Thorsvik © National Geographic Society (Middle) Painting by Ken Marschall (Right) Woods Hole Oceanographic Institution
Back Cover: (Top and Bottom) Paintings by Ken Marschall
Back Flap: Perry Thorsvik © National Geographic Society

Page 2: Ken Marschall Collection
 3: Ken Marschall painting, David Felstein Collection
4–5: Painting by Ken Marschall, David Hobson Collection
6–7: Painting by Ken Marschall
 8: Author's Collection
 9: (Left & right) John Donnelly, author's collection
10: Chris Sauder Collection
11: (Top left) *The Shipbuilder* (Top right and middle) Ken Marschall Collection (Bottom) Harland & Wolff
12: (Cutaway) Courtesy of Anne Tantum (Top) Joseph Carvalho Collection (Bottom) *The Cork Examiner*
13: (Top and middle left) *The Shipbuilder* (Top right) F. Browne, C. Haas/J. Eaton Collection (Bottom right) Courtesy of Jeremy Nightingale
14: (Left) Harland & Wolff (Middle and right) Ken Marschall Collection
15: (Left) Father F. Browne, C. Haas/J. Eaton Collection (Right) Harland & Wolff
16: (Inset top) Courtesy of Ruth Becker Blanchard (Top & bottom) Byron Collection, Museum of City of New York.
17: (Inset top) *Titanic* Historical Society (Top) Harland & Wolff (Bottom) Byron Collection, Museum of City of New York.
18: *The Illustrated London News*
19: (Top) Ken Marschall painting, Dennis Kromm Collection (Middle) Joseph Carvalho Collection (Bottom) *The Illustrated London News*
20–21: Illustrations by Pronk&Associates

22: (Left) *The Illustrated London News* (Top right) Ken Marschall Collection (Bottom right) *The Shipbuilder*
23: Ken Marschall painting, Kenneth Smith Collection (Inset) Illustration by Pronk&Associates
24: (Top) The Mariner's Museum, Newport News, VA (Bottom) The Bettmann Archive
25: Ken Marschall painting, Charles Heebner Collection
26–27: Painting by Ken Marschall, Joseph Ryan Collection
28: Walter Lord Collection
29: (Top left) Walter Lord Collection (Bottom left) The Bettmann Archive (Inset right) Donald Lynch Collection (Right) Ken Marschall Collection
30: Emory Kristof © The National Geographic Society
31: Illustration by Pronk&Associates
32: (Left) Harland & Wolff (Right) Robert D. Ballard
33: Emory Kristof © National Geographic Society
34: Emory Kristof © National Geographic Society (Bottom) Woods Hole Oceanographic Institution
35: (Left) Emory Kristof © National Geographic Society (Right) Illustration by Pronk&Asssociates
36: Robert D. Ballard (Inset) Harland & Wolff
37: (Top) Robert D. Ballard (Inset top) Ray Lepien Collection (Bottom) J. Bailey © National Geographic Society
38: Perry Thorsvik © National Geographic Society
39: Illustration by Pronk&Associates
40: Perry Thorsvik © National Geographic Society
41: Painting by Ken Marschall
42: (Left) Painting by Ken Marschall (Right top) Harland & Wolff (Bottom) Woods Hole Oceanographic Institution
43: (Top left) Harland & Wolff (Right & bottom) Woods Hole Oceanographic Institution
44: Painting by Ken Marschall

45: Painting by Ken Marschall (Inset left) Bill Sauder Collection (Inset right) Woods Hole Oceanographic Institution
46: Painting by Ken Marschall
47: (Top and middle left) Woods Hole Oceanographic Institution (Bottom left) Illustration by Pronk&Associates (Right) Joseph Carvalho Collection
48: Woods Hole Oceanographic Institution
49: (Left) Painting by Ken Marschall (Inset left) F. Browne, C. Haas/J. Eaton Collection (Top right) Ken Marschall Collection (Bottom right) Woods Hole Oceanographic Institution
50–51: Painting by Ken Marschall (Inset photos) Woods Hole Oceanographic Institution
52–53: Painting by Ken Marschall (Color inset photos) Woods Hole Oceanographic Institution (Bathtub) Harland & Wolff (Statue) Howard Holtzman Collection
54: (Left) Donald Lynch Collection (Inset) The Margaret Strong Museum (Right) Woods Hole Oceanographic Institution
55: (Right and inset bottom) Woods Hole Oceanographic Institution (Inset top) F. Sangorski & G. Sutcliffe Ltd.
56–57: Painting by Ken Marschall (Inset top and top right) Woods Hole Oceanographic Institution (Inset bottom) The Mariner's Museum
58–59: Illustrations by Pronk&Associates
60: Perry Thorsvik © National Geographic Society
61: Woods Hole Oceanographic Institution

Madison Press Books would like to thank the following people for their assistance and advice: Rick Archbold; Harriet Ballard; Roger Barrable; Carolyn Brunton; Joseph Carvalho; Peter Elek; Father Guiney S.J.; Eva Hart; Ed Kamuda and the *Titanic* Historical Society, P.O. Box 53, Indian Orchard, Mass. 01151-0053, U.S.A.; Walter Lord; Don Lynch; Jeremy Nightingale; Joseph Ryan; Bill, Eric and Chris Sauder; Anne Tantum; Bertie Traynor.